EVERYTHING
IS MEANINGLESS

EVERYTHING
IS MEANINGLESS

Simple Steps to Create Purpose, Meaning and Happiness

Foreword by Jack Canfield
Co-creator, *Chicken Soup for the Soul*®

W. E. André

Whealth Builders,™ Inc.
JACKSONVILLE, FLORIDA

This publication is designed to provide general motivational advice. The information herein is intended to provide readers suggestions about ways to reach their goals and change their lifestyles and perspectives to improve their lives. This book does not contain medical or psychological or other advice, and should not be interpreted by the reader as offering such advice. Buying or reading this book does not make you a patient or client of the author.

The author and publisher make no representations or warrantees with respect to accuracy, applicability, fitness, or completeness of the contents of this book. The author and publisher, individually and through their companies, specifically disclaim any and all personal liability, loss or risk incurred as a consequence of the use, either directly or indirectly, of any information in this book. The author and publisher are not engaged in rendering legal, medical or psychological, estate planning, financial or other professional services by publishing this book. If expert assistance is required, the services of a competent professional should be sought.

ISBN 0-9761943-0-9
Library of Congress Control Number: 2005929574
First printing 2005 ■ Printed in Canada

To my wife, Latrese, and my children,

Bibi, Tina, Pouchon, and Kenna

Hope you forever look at the world
with childlike wonder,

One

CONTENTS

Acknowledgments

To Latrese, my wife, beautiful, complex yet simple, artistic, intelligent and loving; thanks for the journey, for keeping me out of my comfort zone.

To my Grandma, Naine, for showing me love and teaching me that success is available to anyone.

To Bianca, Schadée, M. Maximus and Taylor, for the inspiration and the aspirations; I hope you keep singing your own words.

To Hattie Peck, my friend. Without your continued support and undying devotion, this book would not be possible. Thank you for challenging me every day, to live the lessons this book teaches.

To Lynn Skapyak, editor, coach and all around pain in my side, thank you for bringing out Prince Pouchon's voice.

To Martha Wallace, editor, thank you for stepping in and completing the final editing of this work. You are a blessing.

Finally to the Divine, my God, for carrying me through the valley of the shadow of death and for allowing me to experience all that makes me who I am today.

Foreword
by Jack Canfield

Meaningless, meaningless, everything is meaningless says the apostle Solomon. What holds meaning? What is meaning? I'm reminded of a modern couple's tale.

Sarah, a mother of two, is married to John, the quintessential businessman. They meet in college, fall in love and marry a few years later. After years working at a law firm, Sarah decides to venture out on her own, to create her own destiny.

Sarah and John are successful at their contracting business and are expanding to new areas. They are happy together. They have a daughter and a son. The couple works hard, provides for their family and enjoys the finer things in life. The American dream has come true for them.

John continues to seek more wealth. He is convinced fulfillment comes in maintaining the American dream. Sarah feels otherwise. She is feeling empty. There is a sadness, a missing link she cannot reconcile.

This loss or lack of meaning, perhaps, is the most tragic tale of modern life. Depending on their disposition, people will look for meaning in love or wealth. Some are lucky enough to conquer romantic love. A few achieve financial freedom. Fewer still, are able to obtain the combination of romantic love and wealth. To their dismay, they realize the age-old formula, money + love = success, is meaningless.

Most people spend their entire lives searching for meaning. Ironically, "meaning"—the first step in the pursuit of happiness—is often the last step taken.

This is possibly the most influential handbook you will ever read. Set on a breathtaking Caribbean island, this is the ancient story of the modern pursuit for meaning, purpose and happiness. Beginning with "delayering" and navigating through the Personal Power Grid, this book promises to take you to unimaginable heights.

If you choose to implement even one of the ideas suggested in this book, your life will be taken to new levels. Apply a few ideas on a daily basis and you could become part of the selected few who have achieved success beyond their most grandiose expectations. As André says, *Do it now ... Go!*

> – Jack Canfield, co-creator,
> *Chicken Soup for the Soul*®

Who is W.E. André?

When I was just ten years old and living in Haiti, before life taught me anything about proper planning and setting self-fulfilling goals, I dreamed of coming to America. My life's success was contingent upon coming to America. I didn't know what I would do there and it didn't really matter. The good life was waiting for me.

Though this was childish thinking, I did something very grown up. I wanted to go to America, so I identified the modes of traveling available to me; boat or plane. Stories of people drowning and being eaten by sharks were too common on the island. I figured a plane was the safer and surer way of getting to America.

The airport was the gateway to heaven. Hope floated in the air. Big, beautiful, friendly airplanes carried people from poverty to riches; from depression to happiness; from oppression to liberty; from death to life.

I went to school and studied hard, hoping one day to board a plane to America. Someday I was going to New York. It was inevitable.

My father, who I never met, was in New York. He had been there, I was told, since before my birth. He sent riches from America to his other kids but never to me; not a letter, not anything. Still, I was going to join him in New York someday. He would send for me.

Marie, my mother, went to America when I was ten years old. I knew my father had secretly sent for her; never mind she'd never heard from him.

Mother had the opportunity to take my sister and me with her. But just as she left me with grandma after I was born, she only wanted to take my sister. The visa dealers told her it was both or none. She chose none. Still I knew the first chance she had she would send for me.

When Mother went to New York, my sister went to live with a cousin on the wealthy side of town. I lived with my abusive uncle in the poor part of the city. Still I knew Mom would send for me to go to America.

Then Grandma went to visit New York. When she returned, she told me all the secrets, "Study hard; everybody in America is smart. Learn how to cook; the women there eat from cans, they don't cook. Learn how to wash your own clothes and dishes and make your own bed."

Grandma had me on an intensive domestic training regimen, preparing me to go to America.

I loved going to the airport. The energy there was uplifting. Any chance I got, whenever someone was going to or coming from America, I went to the airport.

When I was eleven years old I got my first camera. I can still see it. I went to the airport and snapped a perfect picture of an American Airline plane.

That picture became my mantra. I taped it on the wall next to my bed. Every night before going to sleep I stared at it and wondered what it was like in America. Is the ocean blue? Are the stars the same? How high is the highway?

Each morning I looked at my picture and reassured myself that someday I would be waking in New York. I was never deterred. I was always excited. Even when I found out my mother was actively trying to get my sister to America and not me, I still knew I was going to America. It was inevitable.

Sweet sixteen had never been so sweet. My girlfriend was there. Her dress accentuated all her curves, but my teenage mind was focused on America. She had mixed emotions. It was my birthday. It was about noon. My plane was leaving at four o'clock.

Dressed like I just walked off the set of Miami Vice, I climbed the stairs and stepped into an Eastern Airlines plane.

I was on my way to America.

A Familiar Story

"Quickly Mr. André," shouted the nurse, "you're running behind!"

I rushed into the exam room. Mrs. Jones was sitting in a green chair. Her eyes were teary, puffy and red. I noticed her hands trembling. She blew her nose and sobbed quietly.

I must have startled her. She jumped to her feet, threw her shoulders back and firmly shook my hands.

"Good afternoon, Mrs. Jones. Is everything okay? Are you out of your medications again?" I asked.

"No doctor," she managed. She fell back in the green chair, slouched over, tears streaming down her spotted, red cheeks.

"Mrs. Jones, you know I'm a P.A. Why are you crying?"

"It's just that, you know, an old lady my age should be able to take care of herself."

"Mrs. Jones, you are sixty-seven years old and your son is taking good care of you," I protested gently. "You're doing just fine. What is bothering you today?"

Mrs. Jones started to cry uncontrollably. I pulled my stool from under the counter and put my right hand on her shoulder.

"It's going to be okay," I said, reassuringly, "everything will be just fine."

"No it won't, doctor," she protested. "My husband is dead. He left me no money and my son can't even take care of his own family. I went to see a trailer home today and I couldn't even afford the $4,000 it costs to buy it."

As I listened to Mrs. Jones' life story, images of my recent past filled my mind.

Just a few short years ago I came home after a twelve hour workday to find my electricity cut off for the third time in as many months. The melted frost from the freezer leaked a sticky, greenish fluid onto the kitchen floor, making an irritating mess.

I picked up the phone and dialed the power company. "We're sorry," the recording said in a most annoying tone, "this call cannot be completed as dialed. Please check the number and dial again." I did ... several times ... same result.

"*For questions about your bill, call 555-5555.*" I grabbed the light bill, verified the number and dialed it again. Same answer. In my frustration I dialed my friend's number to vent and the same recording came on. That's when it hit me; my phone was disconnected.

As I wallowed in self-pity, I could not understand what had gone wrong. I managed to find enough money and drove to the nearest billing office. With the minimum payment and a promise to pay the balance in a few days, the phone and lights were back on.

Click! White noise emanated from the television. Oh well, my Direct TV had been cancelled. My wife had a tape in the VCR, *Self-esteem and Peak Performance* by Jack Canfield. I turned it on and started watching with no particular interest. The guy was talking about some nonsense and was making promises I knew he could not deliver.

In what I thought was a desperate attempt to find work, my wife and I had been going to the public library and checking out self-help books, videos and tapes. So far they had been useless. Since I had nothing else to do, I watched the entire video once, twice, three times and then some.

By the time I went to bed, early the next morning, I was determined to find and follow my path in life; my purpose.

Thus began my journey in personal development and …

———

"What do you think I should do?"

Mrs. Jones' voice yanked me out of my thoughts. She was calm, her vital signs had returned to normal and the redness had disappeared from her cheeks.

We spoke for a few minutes about life and its tribulations. Then I did the unthinkable; the kind of stuff they warn you about in professional training. I handed twenty dollars to Mrs. Jones and gave her a hug. She smiled and thanked me a million times. She cried, again.

As she signed out at the front desk, I realized she wasn't at all upset about the trailer home.

———

Looking at my past, it is incredible that I rose from near bankruptcy to building a million dollar business in just three short years. Then as the money flowed in and the relationships flourished, I began to realize something was missing.

In our society money is valued more than health. We pursue wealth to the detriment of our well-being and that of others. Success, for a lot of us, is defined by material possessions. We strive for the "American dream"; the big house, luxury cars, and huge retirement portfolio.

We spend our lives accumulating wealth yet we do not create the time to enjoy this luxury. Arthritis, ulcers, cancers and heart disease run rampant in our society. The irony of it is, even though money can buy the best healthcare technology has to offer, the best doctors cannot restore what we have spent years abusing.

During my quest for financial, physical and spiritual wellness I have read several excellent books. The information was clearly presented and highly relevant to my situation. But I found many books to be too passive. I wanted something a little more engaging. I wanted account-ability; a call to action. I soon found that if I were to continue on the path to wealth (financial, physical and spiritual) I had to create a system that would hold me accountable. This is the four step system presented to you here.

The book is divided into two parts. Part One is the coming of age story of a young Caribbean prince who would be a great king. He worked hard to find love and financial wealth only to realize something was still missing. Part One of this book chronicles his journey in search of the missing link, and what he discovered.

Part Two consists of the exercises used by the young prince to create his abundant life. They show how to create financial wealth, improve health, build stronger and more meaningful relationships and strengthen self-esteem and spirituality.

As you travel with the young prince, I hope you will become enlightened, motivated and invigorated. But most importantly, it is my wish you will have a "life plan" on hand that you can implement immediately to create abundance.

Part I

Mining for Meaning

Public opinion is a weak tyrant compared with our own private opinion. What a man thinks of himself, that it is which determines, or rather, indicates his fate.

– Henry David Thoreau

1

Humble Beginnings

Many moons ago, on a small tropical island far away in the West Indies, lived a young prince who was destined to become a great king.

The island was affectionately known, the world over, as Porte des Cieux (gate to heaven). Great men and women journeyed to Porte des Cieux in the pursuit of happiness.

White sandy beaches, with tall and curvy coconut trees that soared towards the heavens, lined the island's coasts.

Islanders traveled to the water by foot or by horseback, donkeys and mules. The repeated use of the same pathways created natural trails which eventually became roads linking all the villages of the island.

Every afternoon, the sky turned orange, the sun cooled down and slowly dipped into the ocean. Children gathered at the beach to play, ride and race with the dolphins.

Late at night, young and old sat around wood fires and roasted beetle nuts. The elders stood in the center, next to the crackling flames. They gestured dramatically while they recounted stories about their ancestors and Porte des Cieux's legendary figures.

Young children, cradled in their mothers' laps, watched with wide eyes and open mouths as they listened to the mesmerizing voices of the elders.

"The Mèt dlo (Med-low) lives in underwater houses. He is the wisest mystical figure of all. He captures promising children and raises them for at least one year. Sometimes he keeps them for their entire life. The more gifted the child, the shorter the stay with the Mèt dlo."

———

On the island lived a wise and fair king. Although he was wealthy, the islanders placed flowers at the gates of his castle and brought him gifts. Even travelers from other parts of the world bestowed great offerings upon the wise king for an audience.

The handsome prince lived in his father's castle which towered atop the highest hill in the village.

As legend has it, when the young prince was just a month old, he was captured by the Mèt dlo. He was kept for only a year.

When he returned, the young prince was raised by his father, the wise king, and his mother, the fair queen. His mother spent all her days by his side. She fed, clothed and read to him from the book of knowledge.

Several servants took care of the young prince and several performers kept him entertained. He had all the nicest garments. He lived a life of splendor and had all his needs met. The wise king spared no expense to make sure his son was well taken care of. In fact, the prince was so well cared for, he became known as Pouchon (beloved).

The incident with the Mèt dlo left the king protective of his son. Prince Pouchon had to spend all his days inside the castle. The court-yard was as far as he was allowed to venture outside his quarters.

As he came of age, the young prince noticed the people around the castle did not all look the same. Some were tall while others were short. Some had long hair while others had none. Some were dark and some were light. Even their garments were different.

Many servants left the castle at night and did not return until the next morning.

Pouchon frowned at his most trusted servant, Géran. "Where do you go when you leave the castle?"

"Oh, I go home, to my castle."

"Why don't you stay at our castle? Don't you like it here?"

"Well of course I do. But I must take care of my kingdom as well."

Prince Pouchon shifted in his golden chair. "I notice some of the children and well, they look different in their clothing."

"Then maybe you should find out more about Porte des Cieux and the people who live there," said Géran returning to his chores.

As each moon passed the young prince observed the coming and going of the servants, the guards, the entertainers and everyone else who visited the castle. He consistently quizzed Géran about the village and the villagers.

"I can tell you about it," said the servant, "but that would not satisfy your curiosity. You need to experience it firsthand."

The curious young prince knew he was not allowed to leave the castle. His father would be upset. He sat in his room and rehearsed how to ask his papa to allow him to go out to the village. "Father, I find myself wondering a lot about the village and the people who live there …"

"So why don't you go and see for yourself," whispered a deep voice behind him.

"Huh?" Prince Pouchon turned around to find his father standing in the doorway. Their eyes locked.

"You may go, but you must refrain from visiting the 'enchanted' side of the village," said the king. He left as quietly as he came.

"The enchanted side?" said the young prince under his breath. "I must find out about that!"

After a few days of preparation and anticipation, the journey began. The young prince kept pace ahead. Every few moments he glanced back and gestured with his hands to Géran to catch up.

An hour and seven kilometers later they arrived at the village. Prince

Pouchon swung one leg over his horse and hopped off. He marched toward the largest castle. Then he skipped across the road to the smallest castle. The young prince reached down and picked a red flower. He handed it to a young princess playing in front of the seventh castle.

He strolled through the village and pulled his horse behind him.

"Do you want to play soccer with me?" a young villager called out to Prince Pouchon.

"No!" screamed the little princess. "He wants to jump rope. Don't you?" she asked, turning to the prince.

They jumped rope, kicked around soccer balls and ran around the corn fields. The young prince spent the entire day playing with the children and visiting with the villagers. By the time he and Géran reached the village center it was already late in the afternoon. Pouchon was tired.

"What do you know about the 'enchanted side?' "

"Only that poverty, both physical and spiritual, runs rampant there," said Géran.

At sunset the prince and his most trusted servant started on their way back to the castle. As they rode, the young prince grew aware that something was amiss.

"This is not the same road we traveled this morning," he said, concerned.

"You're right. It's not."

"What is wrong with the trees here? What happened to their branches?"

"There are not many trees on this side of the village," said Géran.

"I noticed. And look at their branches; they are hanging down as if they have given up hope. They look ready to fall off and die."

Prince Pouchon paused for a moment, turned to his most trusted servant and asked squarely, "Is this ..."

"Yes it is," interrupted Géran.

Young children trampled over each other running towards the prince's horse.

"Gimme some one dola pou mal pocket to shop," they screamed.

"What are they saying?"

"They are begging for something to eat my young prince."

"Why are these children begging on the side of the road, don't they have food at home?"

"Look at their clothes. They are soiled and ragged. These children may not even have a home," said Géran.

The prince's cheeks flushed and his voice broke. "How can they not have a home? And what is that look in their eyes?"

He got off his horse and walked slowly to a young villager. He knelt in front of the little girl. Her face felt cold to his touch. He examined the pointed roundness of her stomach. The young prince ran his finger over her ribs as if to count them.

She stared at him through big, empty brown eyes. With both hands she reached out and wiped his tears.

"Can I have something to eat?" she begged.

"Get away from the stranger," said an obese man. He gestured for the children to move away. The fat man had a large wound on his right leg.

"Sorry," he said, limping toward the young villagers.

"We must go, my young prince," said Géran.

"Is this what you meant by poverty? Are those children poor?"

The most trusted servant nodded.

"That little girl had nothing to eat yet she wiped away my tears," said Pouchon.

"She may be poor, but she is rich in spirit," said Géran.

With his head down, Prince Pouchon pulled his horse behind him and trekked up the hill. Dark frameless images of the poor villagers flashed in front of his eyes.

The king met them at the gates of the castle. One look at his son and he knew.

"So you visited the enchanted side?" he said.

"I feel like I've been beaten up by the mightiest buccaneer of the land," said Prince Pouchon, as he quietly walked to his quarters.

Days came and went. Prince Pouchon wondered what he could do to help the poor villagers. Although his father the wise king was wealthy, the troubled young prince felt poorer than the poorest pauper on the island. All was there for him just for the asking, but somehow Prince Pouchon did not feel entitled.

The prince barely ate. He slept all the time. Nothing consoled him. Nothing brought joy to his soul.

The wise king issued a decree: anyone who cheered up his son would receive two carriages full of treasures.

All the great entertainers from all over the island tried to amuse the young prince, but not one made him smile. The best magicians, charlatans and healers did not bring him out of his depressive state.

Then one day a very old woman visited the king.

"There is an old peasant who has a history of doing great wonders when everyone else failed," she told the king.

On an early Saturday morning with gray skies and the sun hiding behind the clouds, tall and muscular servants loaded two carriages full of bounty.

Two guardsmen, with strong hands and with faces that had never seen a smile, carried Prince Pouchon to the courtyard and placed him in one of the carriages. The young prince did not ask where he was going.

He looked up at the gray sky and felt the heaviness of the air crushing down on his chest. His lungs worked extremely hard to get oxygen to his heart. He went inside his head and made dark frameless images of life.

At the old peasant's home, Prince Pouchon was placed in a room with no furniture. Two floor mats were laid in the center. As he sat down, a slender servant walked in and handed him a wooden cup.

"Drink!" she ordered. "The Wiseman will be with you soon."

A few moments later a white-haired man strolled into the room. He raised his pants legs, crossed his right leg over his left and squatted next to the prince.

"Gentil is my name," the Wiseman said calmly.

Prince Pouchon didn't respond.

"They tell me you have left us for another place."

Again, no response; the young prince stared straight ahead as if he were alone in the room.

"Um, do you mind if I join you in that special place where you are right now?" continued Gentil.

Still Prince Pouchon said nothing.

They sat together not speaking a word, looking into nothingness. The prince stared straight ahead, his shoulders slumped, his breathing slow and shallow.

Gentil looked over at Pouchon. He observed his breathing, his posture and his muscle tone. He then assumed the exact same position as the young prince. Gentil became his complete mirror image.

A few moments passed and they remained sitting quietly. After a while Gentil slowly leveled his shoulders. Prince Pouchon did the same. A few moments later Gentil turned to the prince and smiled at him. Pouchon smiled back. Then ever so softly Gentil spoke, "What do you think is going to help you feel better?"

Prince Pouchon looked up to his right as though searching for an answer; then down to his left as if he were discussing something with himself.

"I want to become successful …"

"What is success to you?" interrupted Gentil.

Images of his father, the wise king, and his castle, flashed in Pouchon's mind. He covered his eyes as if to shelter them from the sparkling gold ornaments. He heard the horses neigh. The young prince rubbed his right thumb over his index and middle finger. He felt the texture of his father's garments. In his mind's eye, he saw the servants carry water to the castle, tend to the animals and trim the trees in the courtyard.

"Success is having lots of treasures, not my father's but my own."

The old Wiseman slowly rose up on his feet and disappeared outside the door. Within a few moments he returned and handed an object to the young prince. Dust flew in the air as Prince Pouchon unwrapped the item. It was a book.

"*Ancient Wisdom for Creating Wealth.* What is this?"

"That is the path to wealth. Go, and be successful."

The skies were blue and the sun was bright. The melodious chirping of the birds gyrated between Pouchon's ears. A warm feeling raced from his lower back to the top of his head, culminating in an explosion inside his brain. Prince Pouchon punched and kicked the air.

"Finally I have figured out what I want out of life."

2

Ancient Wisdom for Creating Wealth

1. Set compelling goals.
2. Visualize your success.
3. Believe in yourself (positive self talk).
4. Check your values.
5. Identify your needs and your resources.
6. Take right action.
7. Be constant and consistent.

How to Set Compelling Goals

"People don't plan to fail, but rather they fail to plan." Goal setting is the key to success.

When goals are properly set, they act as a magnet pulling you toward your desired outcome. It is essential to set compelling goals.

Basic Goal Setting Questionnaire

+ Where are you now?

+ Where do you want to be?
    State your goals in positive terms.
    Be thorough and specific.
    What do you really want?

+ What will you see, hear and feel when you achieve your goal?
    Is your goal compelling?
    Does it pull you?

+ Do a balance check.
    Does your goal fit your belief system?
    What will you gain?
    What will you give up?

As you answer these questions, notice how your body responds in terms of images, sounds and feelings.

+ Finally, do the Cartesian Logic.
    What will happen if you achieve your goal?
    What will happen if you don't achieve your goal?
    What won't happen if you achieve your goal?
    What won't happen if you don't achieve your goal?

Prince Pouchon read the handbook, *Ancient Wisdom for Creating Wealth* in just two days. He read it a second time, paying close attention to any particular message he may have missed during the first reading. Then he read it again.

He followed the guidelines laid out in the handbook. The young prince took an inventory of his financial standing.

Where are you now?	Where do you want to be?
No house	Own my own castle
No treasure	Carriages of gold
No horse	10 horses
No servant	5 servants
No entertainer	5 entertainers

Then he created a mental picture of what he would see, hear and feel when he achieved his goals. He saw the castle. The carriages overflowed with gold. The servants cared for him and his healthy and strong horses. Five performers kept him entertained.

The young prince dedicated the first five minutes of each morning reading and visualizing his goals.

When I achieve my goals I will see:

I see a castle built on two acres of land. The horses live in the quarter acres barn in the back of the castle.

I will hear:

I hear the birds chirping, the servants moving about, the entertainers playing music.

I will feel:

I feel like I'm in control. I feel secure.

Then he did a balance check. Prince Pouchon made certain his beliefs about money did not interfere with his desire to create fortune.

Does your goal fit your belief system?

I believe it is good to make money.

I believe money should be shared.

I believe money does not make me who I am.

What will you gain?

I will gain financial independence.

I will gain ability to give more.

What will you have to give up?

I will lose some friendships.

I will have to give up some time.

Finally the young prince answered the following questions.

What will happen when I achieve my goal?

I will have everything I want.

What will happen if I don't achieve my goal?

I will not have what I want. I will not be able to share with others.

I will remain poor.

What won't happen if I achieve my goal?

I will not be poor.

I will not want for anything.

What won't happen if I don't achieve my goals?

I will not have my castle, my servants, my horses.

Prince Pouchon wrote a one year plan. Then he broke it down into ninety days, thirty days and finally a daily outcome.

One Year Plan

Have a castle on the east side of the village on 10 acres of land in

exactly 365 days.

The castle will have 15 rooms

have 5 servants

have 5 entertainers

have 10 horses

a ½ acre barn

A waterfall

7 carriages of gold

A garden of flowers, coconut trees and mango trees

Achieve financial independence

Ninety Day Plan

Pick location for my castle

Start a business

Start saving

Find other possible sources of income

Thirty Day Outcome

Decide on type of business to start

Decide location of business

Write business plan

Find money to start a business

Identify multiple sources of income

Prince Pouchon followed his plan consistently. He persisted in his endeavor to create wealth. Every morning he spent time visualizing his dreams and his goals. He worked diligently from sunrise to sunset.

When the prince met his thirty day goals, he set a new thirty day outcome. He repeated the process every thirty days for one year.

At the end of the first year, the prince lived in his castle on ten acres of land. Ten servants took care of his needs. Every day he went to his barn and helped the servants groom his ten horses.

The wealthy young prince implemented his plans day after day, year after year. He never once ceased to visualize wealth. Every time he met his goals he set new ones. Three years later he had created seven times more wealth than he had imagined.

Prince Pouchon returned to the enchanted side where he built several castles for the homeless. He fed and clothed many children. To his dismay that did not improve conditions for the long term. It seemed money, though necessary, was not the only solution to their problems.

Soon after, the wealthy prince moved back to his dark world. He spent most of his days in bed.

"Wealth is not fulfilling," he said.

At his father's pleading Prince Pouchon went to see Gentil again.

"What do you think is going to help you feel better this time?" Gentil asked.

The prince pondered the question.

"Maybe if I could become *really* successful," he said.

"What is real success to you?"

Pouchon looked up to his left as though he was trying to remember something. He saw images of the villagers with their mates. He saw them smiling, sharing time together and being happy. He'd thought about this before but never acted on it.

"Maybe real success to me is to have a wonderful mate," he said.

"Take this." Gentil handed him a small booklet, *Love, Sex and Relationships*. "Go, take a mate and be successful."

Prince Pouchon left Gentil feeling excited and hopeful. "This time I have really figured out what I want out of life," he thought.

He returned home looking and acting like a brand new man. The wealthy young prince had no idea what to expect in a relationship. So he read Gentil's booklet.

3

Love, Sex and Relationships

The Love Matrix

Love is often confused with other emotions evoked by desires for affection, togetherness or sex.

In order to experience love, people use matrices. A love matrix is the combination of images, sounds and feelings that must be present in order for someone to experience love.

The process Lunel uses to fall in love with Nadia is different from the process used by Pradel to fall in love with Nadege. No two experience love in exactly the same way. No two love experiences are ever the same. Each comes with its unique characteristics.

People fall in love when part, or their entire love matrix, is matched. When there is a mismatch, they fall out of love.

Deciphering Your Love Matrix

We experience the world through our senses: what we see (S), what we hear (A), and what we feel (M). S stands for sight. A is auditory and M represents movement, what we experience through touch, taste and smell.

Step One

✦ Think of a time when you felt strongly attracted to someone: who, when, and where? _____

_____

✦ In what part of your body did you experience the feeling of attraction? _____

✦ Describe the feeling. _____

✦ What brought on that feeling?

    S)   Was it something you saw? _____

    A)   Was it a sound you heard? _____

    M)   Was it a touch, smell or taste? _____

✦ Which one came first (S, A, M)?

_____ is my attraction pattern.

Step Two

✦ Think of a situation when you experienced love: who when, where? _____

_____

✦ In which part of your body did you experience love?

_____

✦ Describe the experience of love. _____

_____

✦ What brought on that sensation?

    S)   Was it something you saw? _____

    A)   Was it a sound you heard? _____

    M)   Was it a touch, smell or taste? _____

✦ In order of importance, list what must be present for you to fully
experience the feeling of love.

_____ S) Sight

_____ A) Sounds

_____ M) Touch/smell/taste/action

Insert the number that corresponds with your choices.

✦ I experience love first through _____ then _____ and finally _____ .

✦ My love matrix is _____ , _____ , _____ .

How to Find Your Ideal Mate

When looking for the ideal mate you must first determine your attraction pattern. What initially attracts you to someone? Is it *S*, *A* or *M*?

Suppose Pradel's attraction pattern is *sound* (A) and his love matrix
is *sound*, followed by *action* and then *sight* (AMS). He will know he's
drawn to a person when he falls in love with the way she speaks.
The tone and volume of her voice, then the way she moves as she
speaks and finally, how she looks, determine whether she matches his
attraction pattern.

Once you know your pattern then you must find out how someone
can match it. You must determine if the person follows part or your
entire love matrix. Is it a fit?

For example a person who experiences love by sight + sound + touch
(SAM) enters into a relationship with a person who shows love by touch
+ sound + sight (MAS). In order for him to experience complete love,
his mate must show it visually, then with sounds and finally through
movement (touch, taste, smell, action).

The ideal mate is the person who, meticulously, follows every detail
on your love matrix. Every behavior has to model your love matrix.
There can be no compromising. That will only lead to later strife.

For example, Isaac is AMS. He enters in a relationship with Nadege who is SMA. She complains he is too messy (S), works too much and doesn't spend enough time with her (M). He claims she nags him (A).

Matching your attraction pattern is what draws you to a person. Modeling your love matrix is what keeps you there.

Communicating in a Relationship

Communication is the key to a successful liaison. Yet the secret to the effective exchange of information is not so apparent. Perhaps it is the fact that the secret is so fundamental.

Great communicators have good relationships. Conveying ideas by modeling the love matrix creates blissful and long-lasting unions. To easily relate to people, speak their language. Relay your message in a manner they understand.

Imagine you have to talk to someone whose native tongue is different from yours. Though you may manage to convey your message, you will greatly improve rapport with the person when you learn his language.

Speaking the same idiom, does not equate to effective communication. It is not what is said but how it is said that conveys the message. People tend to communicate using the same strategy they draw on to experience love.

Paul's love matrix is SAM. In most instances, he speaks using that same model. To relate to him, speak his native language, his love matrix. It is not enough to say, "I love you," to him. You must first look in his eyes sincerely (S), then say, "I love you" in a heartfelt tone (A) and finally touch him (M).

How to Have a Sex-filled Marriage

Sex is a major part of any successful marriage. Without it, even the best union withers and dies.

The desire for sex, or togetherness, is one of the most powerful emotions experienced by mankind. Many wise men and women have jeopardized their lives to fulfill sexual desires.

Sex is a healthy and necessary part of any successful marriage. Misinformation and ambiguous rhetoric about sexuality have created a cloud of distrust around the subject.

It is neither true that women are not interested in sex, nor that men only think of sex. The awareness and understanding of these facts can greatly improve sexual relations in a marriage.

When you are aware of your mate's attraction pattern it is wise to use it for matters related to the bedroom. Men and women often complain that their mate spends the entire day at work or play then expects them to be ready for sex at a moment's notice. This type of behavior will lead to dissatisfaction and can eventually destroy the best of marriages.

Sex becomes a chore only when a partner's love matrix is not being followed.

Pay close attention to the little matters relating to sex. Apply the love matrix in every step. A person, like Paul, who experiences love through a SAM model should be made love to following that exact model. The foreplay should begin with visual stimulation, followed by sound, culminating in touch and movement.

Each action must follow that exact sequence; whether it is a kiss, a touch or a sound. An illusion of sight, sound and touch must be created at each step of the love making moment.

Every detail must follow that exact model. A person whose love matrix is SMA will enjoy mostly visual stimulation, followed by touches, then sounds.

How to Create Everyday Romance

You would think if you know your partner's attraction pattern and read her love matrix; it would be a simple task to create romance in your relationship. Sadly, the opposite is often true.

Romance is the combination of love and sex. It is the deeper manifestation of affection through the fulfillment of your mate's love matrix.

To create romance, identify your mate's love matrix. Model that matrix to the best of your ability, every waking moment of the day and night. If your mate is primarily visual, show your love visually. Keep a clean environment. Take care of your looks.

✦ A sight (S) person may prefer beauty.

✦ An individual with sound (A) as a main strategy needs to hear reaffirming words.

✦ Someone who is primarily (M) enjoys physical contact, gifts or any action of closeness.

This is not an exhaustive manual. It is designed to help you plant the right seed to grow a fruitful relationship.

———

"Are you busy?"

Géran almost jumped out of his sweaty, mahogany-colored skin. "You startled me, Prince Pouchon."

"I saw you sitting here. I thought we could talk for a moment."

"Oh sure, I like the center court. It's the only place where I feel at peace."

The young prince looked at Géran with concern. "Are you happily married?"

"I'm very happy. Why do you ask?"

"Well, it looks like relationships are more complicated than I thought."

"Did you read the book?"

"*Love, Sex and Relationships*? I did, and I have it with me. But I am more confused now than before I read it," said Pouchon.

"What exactly is confusing you?"

"The SAM Code. It is a great idea but some of it does not make sense to me. For example, I see S means sight. I understand A means auditory. But what is M?"

"Okay, see if you can follow this. S stands for images; what we see with our eyes. A represents sounds; what we hear with our ears. M symbolizes movement; what we feel through touch, taste, smell and anything physical, like movement and posture."

"Wait, movement is touch, taste, smell and anything physical? So movement also represents feeling?"

"That's right Prince Pouchon. But it is not emotions."

"I believe that is where my confusion is," said Prince Pouchon. "Forgive me for being naïve, but how does this help me have a successful relationship?"

"You're supposed to use your love matrix to find your ideal mate."

"I guess I should have done the exercise in the book, huh?"

"Let's do it now, Prince Pouchon."

Finding Your Love Matrix

We experience the world through our senses: what we see (S), what we hear (A), and what we feel (M). S stands for sight. A is auditory and M represents movement, what we experience through touch, taste and smell.

Step One

+ Think of a time when you felt strongly attracted to someone: who, when, and where?   _A beautiful princess, while visiting the village for the first time_

+ In what part of your body did you experience the feeling of attraction?   _In my chest_

✦ Describe the feeling. _____

      I feel a deep, bottomless sensation in my chest .

✦ What brought on that feeling?

    S)   Was it something you saw?   _____

    A)   Was it a sound you heard?   _____

    M)   Was it a touch, smell or taste? _M_

✦ Which one came first (S, A, M)?

    _M_ is my attraction pattern.

Step Two

✦ Think of a situation when you experienced love:

who when, where? _____

      An entertainer, two years ago, in the castle courtyard

✦ In which part of your body did you experience love?

    In my chest

✦ Describe the experience of love. _____

      A deep, bottomless, expanding sensation in my chest

✦ What brought on that sensation?

    S)   Was it something you saw?   _____

    A)   Was it a sound you heard?   _____

    M)   Was it a touch, smell or taste? _M_

✦ In order of importance, list what must be present for you to fully experience the feeling of love.

    _2_   S) Sight

    _3_   A) Sounds

    _1_   M) Touch/smell/taste/action

Insert the number that corresponds with your choices.

✦ I experience love first through __M_ then __S_ and finally __A_ .

✦ My love matrix is __M_ , __S__ , __A__ .

"Now you know your attraction pattern."

"I am a strong M," said the young prince.

"So you're Movement oriented. What is your love matrix?"

"I am MSA. I am attracted by action then by what I see and finally what I hear."

They both laughed heartily.

"When you look for your soul mate, make sure she has the same love matrix as you do."

⸻

The young prince continued to study the manual thoroughly. After three months, he went to his father's castle and declared, "I am ready to take a mate!"

Soon everyone in the village knew Prince Pouchon was about to get married. The word spread like wildfire.

As is the custom on this beautiful tropical island, when a young prince decides to take a mate, his father holds a grand Caribbean gala so the prince can meet and select his princess.

All the eligible young maidens were invited to attend. The news traveled far and wide all over the island. An aura of excitement and expectancy floated in the tropical air.

The gala was a great success. A few young maidens matched Pouchon's attraction pattern. But he did not pick a mate. He needed more time to find someone who met his love strategy. He wanted to find his soul mate.

The wise king was frustrated. "How dare he embarrass this family? How dare he not choose his mate?"

"Love cannot be hastened," said the fair queen. "How long did it take you to find me?"

"You are the voice of reason, my lady. I will go talk to my son."

Pouchon sat alone in the center court pondering the matter at hand. He was disappointed he did not find his ideal mate. It is unheard of for a prince to not choose his mate at the gala. This was the usual way of doing things. The young prince worried his father might be upset.

"Are you alright?" The deep voice was unmistakable.

"I am alright father. I hope I did not disappoint you."

"This is about you, son. Just so you know, I did not choose your mother at the gala."

"Really? You mean … how did you find her?

"I used the book."

"It did not seem to help me tonight."

"Maybe you did not use it properly, son. Were you attracted to any princesses at the gala?"

"Yes, but as soon as I approached them I realized they were not for me."

"How is that?"

"They met my attraction pattern but not my love matrix."

"Your attraction pattern is M and your love matrix is MSA, right?"

"How did you know?"

"How long have you been my son? It is my duty to know. Now, how are you using the attraction pattern?"

"I am not sure what you mean, father."

"What attracts you to a princess?"

"I am attracted to the way she carries herself."

"What about that attracts you, son?"

"She has to move gracefully."

"What is graceful?"

"It is in the way she moves, the way she carries herself, the way she looks and then the way she talks."

"Is that in order of importance, son? She has to move gracefully, look graceful, and talk graciously?"

"That is the exact order."

"What have you noticed about that order?"

Prince Pouchon thought for a moment. She has to *move* gracefully, *look* graceful and *talk* graciously.

"Oh, wow! My attraction pattern follows my love map."

"What do you mean when you say she has to move gracefully?"

"Her movements have to be well coordinated, visually pleasing and musical, if that makes sense."

"Do you realize the pattern you used in describing her movements, son?"

"I used my love map. I did not adhere to it during the gala. I wanted to please everyone so I looked for any reason to pick a mate. I did not want to seem particular."

"If there is ever a time to be selective, son, this is it. When you hold fast to your love strategy you cannot fail. Your soul mate will match your love map down to the smallest detail; just like I have just shown you."

"What do I do now, father?"

"Go get some rest. Do not worry about finding your ideal mate. When the time is right, you will find each other."

A year later, Prince Pouchon met a beautiful young princess from the enchanted side. She had no material riches but she was rich in spirit. She moved gracefully and took great care of herself. She enjoyed spending time with him and spoke words that bolstered his esteem.

The young princess was attracted by the adventure in Pouchon's eyes. She felt power in the way he walked and heard strength in the words he spoke. Butterflies swarmed in her belly. He matched her love strategy perfectly. She was to become his mate.

Soon they were married in what was the grandest Caribbean royal wedding of all time. The islanders would be talking about it for a long time to come. Their honeymoon was pure nirvana. Within a year the happy couple had twin children, a beautiful boy and a lovely girl. Life was indeed grand.

The new family traveled all over the island. They bought beautiful gold and silver statues and jewels. Prince Pouchon spent time with his children. He fed, bathed and read to them. Every evening after the children were asleep the romantic prince spent time talking to and loving his wife.

One day the young prince woke with a strange, yet familiar, empty sensation in his gut. It had been seven years since he experienced that feeling. He went inside his head to figure out what was happening to him.

It was that old dark place again racing to catch up with him. The darkness approached quickly, ready to engulf him.

"I have it all. There could not possibly be anything else out there. I have experienced love, treasures, travel and all the riches the island has to offer."

Pouchon covered his face with both hands. "Why do I feel so empty? The mystery of life confuses me."

The young prince felt discouraged. The path ahead seemed bleak and without meaning. He felt he needed a breakthrough, a step in the right direction.

One morning, the family woke to find Prince Pouchon gone. He went to seek an audience with Gentil one more time.

4

Mining for Purpose

"I've been expecting you," said Gentil as he beckoned the prince to come sit next to him.

He took a seat beside Gentil and sighed heavily. His face was somber, his breathing shallow and his body limp.

The slender servant walked into the room with a golden tea set, placed it on the floor and poured them tea. Gentil handed the prince a golden cup and they sipped tea together.

"Thank you," Pouchon mouthed to the servant.

It was the same servant who brought him tea the first time he went to see Gentil.

"Are you successful yet?" Gentil asked, already knowing the answer.

"Alas, I've done everything I can but I remain unsuccessful. I come here today seeking your counsel; maybe you may shed some light on this impasse."

"If I may," interjected the servant, "it sounds like you've done everything you've set out to do. Yet you're not fulfilled. Maybe you ought to examine your meaning of true success."

Prince Pouchon seemed surprised. He nodded respectfully.

"What does it mean to you to be successful? Go inside your mind and tell me, what do you really want?" continued the servant.

"Meaningless, everything is meaningless," lamented the prince.

"What holds meaning for you?"

"I want to find out what I should be doing with my life. Why am I here?"

"You are here to fulfill your destiny," said the servant.

"What is my destiny?"

"Your destiny is your life's purpose."

"How do I find my purpose?"

"I want you to think back to when you were a little child. Write down one hundred and one things you dreamed of accomplishing," she directed.

The young prince glanced over at Gentil who nodded for him to proceed. He had never taken the time to examine his life's purpose. A frown formed on his forehead.

"How far back do you want me to go?"

"As far back as you can remember. Go back to the first time you can recall having aspirations."

"One hundred and one aspirations! That sounds like a lot."

"You mean to tell me you can't think of one hundred and one things you wanted to do since you were a child?"

"Well it just sounds like a lot," said Prince Pouchon.

"Write about the little things, like learning how to swim, going swimming with the dolphins, maybe you can write about what kind of family you wanted, the ideal mate you dreamed of, how many children you wanted or what kind of castle you wanted to have."

"Well, if I write about that I will have well over a hundred and one aspirations."

"Excellent," said the servant. "Be sure to include your aspirations about wealth, health, love and spirituality. Do it now!"

Prince Pouchon started right away on his task. He made a diagram to help him categorize his list.

Health

Learn how to swim

Learn how to ride a horse

Be strong

Grow tall

Be a medicine man

 Wealth

Be like my dad

Have a huge castle

Have many entertainers

Have lots of gold

Have many carriages

 Love

Be married

Have children

Have many friends

Be loved

Make my father proud

 Spirituality

Go to heaven

Meet God

Have magical powers

Know the future

Live forever

The wealthy young prince went inside his mind, back to his early days. The earliest he could remember thinking about what he wanted to do was at age five. He wrote fervently. A few moments later he announced that he completed his task. He had his list of one hundred and one dreams.

"Excellent," said the servant. "I want you to write down one hundred and one things you want to do now. Take your time and dream big. If you could do anything you want to do, what would you be doing? If you knew you could not fail, what would you try to do?"

The young prince went back to work. He liked the idea of dreaming big.

"Hmm," he thought, "what would I try, if I knew I could not fail?"

He wrote fervently and before long categorized his one hundred and one dreams into four sections: health, wealth, love and spirituality.

"I have completed my work," said Pouchon proudly.

"Now compare your two lists. Note how they are similar; see how they are different," said the servant.

Prince Pouchon peered at his lists, noting the similarities. "I just realized something," he exclaimed. "Though I no longer want to be a medicine man, my desire to help people has not changed. I just want to do it in a different way."

He was amazed to realize the resemblance between the two.

The servant looked at him knowingly. "What you'll find is most people have certain desires that feel natural to them."

"So although I may find different ways of fulfilling them, my underlying desires or needs will remain the same."

"That's right. Most people make up their minds at a very early age what they want to accomplish in life. They have goals and they know how to reach them," explained the servant.

"I guess, as we go through life, we lose sight of our hopes and dreams," said Prince Pouchon.

"People continuously lower their standards hoping they might reach their goals but they never do. Now I want you to create your power list."

"What is a power list?"

"Write down the items that are similar in your two lists. Then prioritize them in order of importance. Finally, choose the top ten dreams you want to accomplish in this lifetime."

Pouchon created his power list. In it he wrote the similarities between his childhood aspirations and his present dreams. He categorized them from most to least meaningful.

"Look at your power list," instructed the servant. "Within it is your life's purpose."

"My purpose is to find freedom and share it with others," thought Pouchon. "What about my other dreams?" he asked.

"When you find and pursue your purpose, you will fulfill your every desire. Now that you know your life's purpose, what is true success to you? Keep the following questions in mind."

+ Where are you in your life now?
+ Where would you rather be? What do you really want?

+ What will happen if you get what you want?
+ What will happen if you don't get it?

+ Can you get what you want on your own?
+ Who is responsible to help you get it?
+ What's preventing you from getting it?

+ How will you know when you have what you want?
+ Where, when and with who will you be when you get it?
+ What resources will you need to get it?

The young prince went inside his mind for a while. He looked up and to the left, bringing up pictures from his past. Then his eyes went up and to the right, constructing images of how he would like his life to be. Finally, his eyes fluttered down to his left, as he discussed with himself the life he wanted to live.

It took him a while but Prince Pouchon answered all the questions. He wrote down his definition of success.

> Success, to me, is the enjoyment of a balanced life with a sense of fulfillment. It is freedom to live out my life's purpose, freedom to be free.

"Now remember, success is different for everyone. Never judge success solely on the outward manifestations of wealth. Never impose your definition of success on other people. Find out what they want to achieve and help them do it," said the servant.

She picked up the tea set and left the room as quietly as she came. Nodding his head, Gentil smiled at the prince.

"There is an old Wise One who lives in the easternmost village. She is outstanding at helping people get started on their journey of success. Go and find her," said Gentil. "She is awareness. Look, listen and feel. It's like my wife just showed you. No one can be successful unless they first become aware."

5

Becoming Aware of Your Inner Power

Who looks outside, dreams;
who looks inside, awakes.

– C. G. Jung

On the Road to Awareness

Action

Responsibility

Understanding

AWARENESS

After leaving the Wise One, Prince Pouchon returned home to his family. Within days he was down in his dark hole again. He was torn between living a life of purpose or taking care of his loved ones. He was slow to realize the two were not mutually exclusive.

"What is wrong with you son? I had to come here to see how you're doing. You have not left your castle in weeks."

"I went to see Gentil."

"I know. Why are you disheartened?"

"I found my purpose in life."

"And that saddens you?"

"No, Father, I am simply baffled. How is it that I finally find my life purpose and it requires me to give up everything I love?"

"That is the price of success, son."

"How am I supposed to care for my family by leaving?"

"How are you going to care for your family if you remain depressed?"

Prince Pouchon sat up on his bed. "I will overcome this. I know it."

"Maybe for a while."

"How is it going to look, leaving my family like this?"

"How is it going to look, to whom? Do you believe that you will benefit your family by living a purposeful life?"

"Yes, Father, I do."

"How did you come to the conclusion that you have to leave?"

"The Wiseman told me to travel east. I have searched for alternatives but it just seems like nothing else will do."

"Are you at peace with that decision, son?"

"I am ... when I am not concerned with what others will think of me."

"Then you know what you must do."

The decision to leave did not come easily.

One evening the young prince spoke to his wife. "I have to go on a journey," he announced.

"Where are you going? How long are you going to be gone?"

"As you know, I have not been feeling fulfilled in the last few moons ..."

"You need to abandon your family so you can be fulfilled?"

"When I went to see the Wiseman he helped me to realize that my purpose in life is to help others."

"Why don't you find some people here in the village to help?"

"I have already traveled that path. I must follow my destiny," said the young prince.

"Why don't you start by helping yourself and your family?"

"That is exactly what I am trying to do."

"You think you're helping, by leaving us?"

"Do you really believe that is what I am doing?"

She cried quietly. "Well you are leaving aren't you?"

"Do you believe that my intentions are less than honorable?"

"No, I don't," she managed between tears. "It's just that you're leaving and we're going to miss you."

Pouchon pulled his wife close to his heart and held her tightly. "I know. I will miss you and the children as well. But this is something I have to do."

"You will not be complete until you find what you seek. I know that it will be easier for you to find it with my support. I wish I could come with you."

Pouchon wiped away her tears.

"I want you to know that my thoughts will always be with you, Pouchon."

"You are a virtuous woman. You are wiser than I am. If I am ever lost, I will use your love as my guide."

The departure date arrived. His pulse raced. His heart pounded in his chest. Though he was nervous, the young prince knew that to grow he had to step outside of his comfort zone.

He took in a deep breath and put his right foot in front of the left. With each step Prince Pouchon grew more confident.

Prince Pouchon left all his possessions and everything that was dear to his heart and started his journey of success.

Many moons passed since the young prince left his life of comfort in pursuit of awareness. The power of purpose led him to the gates of his destiny.

Large mountains surrounded the easternmost village. Tall and majestic trees lined each side of the road, their branches overlapping across the top to form a covered pathway.

The villagers greeted Pouchon openly, with warm smiles.

"Well, good day young prince."

He smiled and answered the same.

The young prince wandered about the village, admiring the scenery.

"Are you lost?" asked a tiny, little voice.

He looked around, but did not see anyone.

"I'm up here," giggled the tiny, little voice.

Pouchon looked up and saw a young princess perched on a large wisdom tree smiling down at him.

He smiled back at her. "I'm looking for awareness."

"If you are looking for awareness, you must go see old Wise One Savante."

"Savante?"

"Uh huh."

She put her thumb under her chin and her index finger on her lip. She looked up as though searching for what to say next.

"I'll show you the way if you carry me on your back." The little princess climbed down the tree and hopped on his back.

"This way," she pointed.

White noise resonated from the waterfall. Fresh air, from the chatting trees filled his lungs. Prince Pouchon felt a sudden wave of calmness. This was a familiar feeling. He had been here before.

As he approached the castle the front door swung open.

"Come in! Come in!" said the old Wise One excitedly. "I've been expecting you."

Surprised, the young prince stuttered. "Uh, uh, I was told you could help me find Awareness. I heard you know her well."

The little princess jumped off the prince's back.

The old Wise One smiled. "Soon you will too. I want you to stay for a while, then I will lead you to her."

Pouchon turned around to thank the little princess but she was already gone.

Daybreak, the roosters crowed. Someone chanted by the waterfall. Prince Pouchon went outside to find Savante sitting erect with her legs folded under her. Long, grayish-white, curly hair covered part of her face.

She sensed his presence and summoned him to sit next to her.

"I've traveled far and wide hoping that you might help me find Awareness," said the young prince.

"In order to find awareness, you must first be awakened."

Prince Pouchon frowned. He was not sure what she meant. "I am awake," he thought.

Reading the confusion on his face she explained, "Being awakened is being conscious of your surroundings. It is the art of living in the here and now. Once you are awakened you will become aware."

Savante handed Prince Pouchon a small booklet.

Becoming Aware of Your Inner Power

Most people are unaware of their full potential. They settle for a mediocre existence when in fact, everything has been provided for them. Being unaware of their power leads them to crawl through life like a reptile, instead of soaring like a Master Executor.

People have the ability to do just about anything they want to do. It is written, in the ancient book of wisdom, we have the ability to command a mountain to move and it will obey. History is full of stories about people who have done just that, but the number who is capable of such a feat remains finite.

To those who want to tap into their inner power, the journey begins with the awareness of their power and the acceptance that the source is within them.

Begin by examining the tools available to create Infinite Power. Every event we experience is stored in the brain. From the moment of birth (some believe from conception) our experiences are sorted, prioritized and stored in little boxes called memory cells located in our mind. Each experience has its own little memory box.

We store our experiences so we can refer back to them when we need guidance. This process is learning. We learn through two mechanisms.

Philosophical learning is the gathering and the processing of information. An adolescent will refrain from sexual activities because he is told it is dangerous.

Behavioral learning is done through trial and error: a baby cries and she gets milk, a child touches hot coal and he gets burned.

To store our experiences, we must first gather them from our environment. Our five basic senses (sight, sound, touch, taste and smell) are the tools used to collect information from our surroundings.

A woman sits in her garden, listens to the soothing sound of the waterfall, admires the blooming flowers, enjoys the warm sun against her skin while savoring the tender aroma and sweet taste of an orange. This experience, gathered using her five basic senses, is now stored in a memory box in her brain.

Once stored, our experiences remain with us for the duration of our lives. They are never deleted. No matter how big or how small, every event is stored in the brain.

The brain stores experiences, in order of importance, to prevent chaos. Information needed on a daily basis is stored in the "daily

routine" memory box. Experiences that are rarely used are cata-
logued in the "just in case" memory box.

When we need information, we retrieve it using the tools we
used to collect it, the basic five senses. Remember the woman who
enjoyed the sweet taste of orange in her garden? She will use all
the same senses to retrieve that information, when she wants to
remember what it is like to enjoy an orange on a sunny day.

The five senses are simplified in a system called the SAM Model;
sight (S), auditory (A) and movement (M). The sense of touch,
taste, and smell are grouped under movement (M). This system
helps us determine how we use our basic senses to collect information about our environment.

The information we gather from our environment using the
SAM model and store in our brain, forms our Personal Power Grid.
It serves as a map to help us navigate through life. When we face a
new situation, we refer to our Personal Power Grid for insight,
through the SAM model.

Daily experiences, beliefs, values and criteria make up the
Personal Power Grid. When our experiences consistently produce
the same outcome, they become beliefs. Some beliefs are philosophical in nature; we have no positive knowledge that they are
true. Values are the things that are important to us. Criteria are the
reasons why we do the things we do.

There are five power positions on our personal power grid.
Self-Power—experiencing the world from one's own point of
view; Other-Power—experiencing the world from someone else's
point of view; Third-Power—experiencing the world from the
point of view of a detached observer; Integral-Power—
experiencing the world from an insider's point of view; and
Infinite-Power—being one with the source.

6

De-layering: The More You Lose the More You Gain

Two days had passed since the young prince read the booklet. His mind could not make sense of it. "Can I ride on your back again?"

Prince Pouchon was trekking up the east mountain, when he heard a familiar voice behind him. He smiled, "Only if you promise not to disappear this time."

The little princess hopped on his back and they made their way up the east mountain and down toward the ocean.

"Are we going to the beach?"

"Uh huh," said the prince distantly.

"So, have you found awareness yet?"

"Not yet, but I am working on it."

"What have you found out so far?"

"Only that I have to use my Personal Power Grid to be awakened."

"You say that as though it's a joke," said the little princess.

"I don't think it is a joke. I just don't know how to proceed," said Prince Pouchon defensively.

The ocean was turbulent. Huge waves crashed on the shores. The little princess jumped off the prince's back and ran toward a bed of rocks. She sat down and gestured for him to join her.

Prince Pouchon threw a small rock in the water. "How do you know so much about awareness anyway?"

"I heard Savante say that if you want to become aware you have to first discover who you are and learn to live in the moment."

"I know exactly who I am. I am a father, a husband, a provider ..."

"That's what everybody always says," interrupted the little princess, "but then Savante teaches them about Over-layering."

"Forgive me, Over-layering?"

"Yeah, it's when people use all these names to explain who they are."

"I guess I'm pretty over-layered, huh?" said Prince Pouchon half-jokingly.

"Savante says that these names describe what people do and not who they are." The little princess looked at the sun.

"I have to go home," she said and began to run toward the village.

"I guess she didn't want me to carry her," thought the young prince, as he followed.

They ran up and down the east mountain until they reached the village. Prince Pouchon accompanied the little princess to a beautiful castle tucked away on a cul-de-sac.

"Will you come in and eat with me?" The little princess grabbed Pouchon's hand and led him inside the castle to a small room, with a table and four wooden chairs. Then she went outside to get water from the well.

Prince Pouchon leaned on the table. Images from the day ran through his mind. A servant came in from an adjacent room.

"A meal is being prepared in the prince's honor and will be ready in a little while," said the servant.

"Are you okay, sir?" asked the servant, noticing the somber look on the prince's face.

"Yes, I'm fine, why do you ask?"

"You look a bit lost," said the servant. "I hope the lil' princess is not putting too much on your plate."

"No, she was just telling me about layering."

"Yes sir, I kinda figured that, sir."

"Really! How is that?"

"Well, I don't want to talk too much, sir, but one time the lil' princess gave me this note but I still can't tell what it means. No sir, I can't."

The servant looked to his left and his right, making sure no one was watching. Then he reached into his back pocket and handed the prince a folded piece of paper.

Pouchon began to read, "Self-discovery begins with the knowledge that we are all created with the same potential ..."

"Not so loud, sir, the walls got ears," said the servant.

Prince Pouchon lowered his voice. "Anything a person can accomplish, I can achieve the same, according to my own abilities. I must realize and believe that all people are created equal; that we can all achieve the same goals in life. We all share the same sea of consciousness. Even our behaviors are basically similar. We all have access to the same resources."

"See what I mean, sir? That don't make no sense. But you didn't hear that from me. No sir, you didn't."

The servant took back the piece of paper and left mumbling under his breath. The little princess came in the room with a basket of vegetables and washed them in a pot of water.

"Let me help you with that," said the prince.

"I like helping to cook. It makes me feel like I contribute," said the little princess.

"Getting back to layering, what else did you hear about it?"

"Why?"

"It is not completely clear to me."

The little princess took a white onion from the basket of vegetables. She paused for a moment then reached for a red onion. She placed both onions on the table.

"What is the difference between these two onions?" she asked.

"One is white and the other is red."

"Now peel both onions until you get to their core," she instructed.

One by one Prince Pouchon peeled each layer. Tears filled his eyes blurring his vision. He sniffled. He cried. But he peeled the onions until he could peel no more.

"Now how are those two onions different?" asked the little princess.

"They are identical at this level."

"It's just like that for people too. This process is called de-layering. When you take away all the layers that people have the only thing left is their core, which is their true self."

"I think I understand. We use names to label all the different things we do. For example, I am a father, a husband, a son, a prince, a seeker, and on and on."

"That's right, Prince Pouchon."

"When I use all these names I create layers. When I take away the layers I am left with just me, my core, which is my true self."

"That's exactly what Savante says," said the little princess.

"I am confused though. How do I remove the layers? How do I take away the fact that I am a father or a son?"

"You don't really have to take it away. Just pretend. Suppose you are no longer a father, does that take away from who you are?"

"Of course not."

"Okay, then how do you feel about no longer being a father?"

"I feel I prefer being a father. I enjoy children but at the same time I do not feel diminished by not being a father."

"Well, try removing each title that you have, one by one until you have none left. And each time that you remove a title, check to see how you feel about losing it."

"What if removing a title bothers me, what should I do?"

"Savante said that if you have trouble letting go of a title, then that means that you have an attachment," answered the little princess.

"Did Savante tell you what an attachment is?"

"It is when a person develops an unhealthy bond to something or someone."

"So once I remove all my layers, I am left with me," said Prince Pouchon.

"That's right, and that is the real you. It is infinite potentiality. At that level, everyone is equal; everyone has the same potential."

"So what Savante is saying is everyone at the core, is the same. Hmm, it is like the old analogy about water."

"What's an 'analogy'?" asked the little princess.

"It is when you use one thing as an example, to explain something else. I once heard a Wise One say that water can exist in many different forms, sizes and shapes. It can be liquid, solid, or gas.

"In the liquid form it takes the shape of any container you put it in. In the solid form you can shape it into anything you desire. But whether it is liquid, solid or gas, water is still water. Its essence does not change."

"Wow!" said the little princess, "I'll never look at water the same way again."

"What the Wise One meant was water in any form is still water. Just like us; when you take away all the names and titles, we are all the same."

"So then Prince Pouchon, what are you left with when you remove all your layers?"

"I am left with me."

"So who are you then?"

"I am," said Prince Pouchon.

They had dinner. The little princess retired. It was already evening when Prince Pouchon finally made it back to Savante's castle. The prince greeted her and he went to the guestroom.

He paced around for a while then decided to go outside. He found Savante sitting on the porch gazing at the stars.

"Shouldn't you be resting?" she asked him without turning around.

"I feel like there are a thousand horses galloping in my mind."

"What is troubling you?"

"Nothing is troubling me. I am just confused about de-layering."

"Exactly what about de-layering is bothering you?"

"I am not really sure I believe that once de-layered, everyone is the same. That would mean I am no different than a common thief," protested the prince.

"Not just a common thief. That means that at your basic core you aren't any different from the wisest king, either."

"How impertinent, you mean to tell me there is no difference between a common thief, a whore or my father, the wise king?" said the young prince indignantly.

"Temper, temper, my young prince!"

"I am not upset. I just want to see your point."

Savante reached into her pocket and pulled out two silver coins equal in value. She placed the coins on the ground in front of Pouchon.

"What do you see is the difference between these two coins?" she asked.

"Well one is new and shiny and the other is old and worn."

"Which one is more valuable?"

The young prince peered at the coins to establish their worth.

"They appear to be equal in value," he answered.

She picked up the old coin and threw it on the muddy ground.

"Which coin is more valuable now?"

Prince Pouchon looked incredulous. "Neither, they are both worth the same. One is muddied and the other is clean."

"So you agree that the mud and the dirt did not reduce the coin's value?"

Prince Pouchon smiled. "Not in the least," he answered.

"Now take the whore, the common thief and the wise king; who is more valuable?"

"The wise king is …" there was a brief moment of silence. Pouchon's eyebrows raised and his pupils widened, "Oh! So if I were to de-layer the whore, the common thief, and the wise king, they would all have the same value."

"How is that possible?" Prince Pouchon continued as though talking to himself. "With the coins, I was able to immediately see beyond the dirt and the mud, to realize the coins were in fact, equal in value. De-layering the whore, the common thief and the wise king allowed me to see them as individuals."

"What happens when you de-layer the individuals themselves?" asked Savante.

The young prince seemed perplexed. "How do you de-layer the individuals?"

"You remove their habits and their behaviors; you must transcend the flesh."

"Transcend the flesh?"

"Yes, you have to go beyond the flesh. Only then will you get to the essence of every human being," said Savante.

"And what is that?"

"That is their core beliefs. Now transcend that and what do you have left?"

"The only thing left is them."

"That is the source, Infinite-Power," said Savante.

Prince Pouchon went back into the guestroom. Before he retired for the night, he summarized what he learned in a journal he had started.

Pouchon's Journal

Every action I take has a positive intent. I am more than my actions. When my titles are removed I am de-layered to the flesh. When I transcend the flesh, I am de-layered to my core beliefs. That is the essence of every human being. When I go beyond my core beliefs, I reach the source. At that level, anything is possible. Everyone shares this same potential.

Using my Personal Power Grid, I realize in Self-Power that I experience the world from one point of view, mine. Any layers I see are self-imposed.

When I shift to Other-Power, I experience the world through someone else's point of view. Any layers from that position are imposed by society.

From Third-Power, I see the world through the eyes of a detached observer. I witness both the self-imposed layers and the layers tagged on by others.

In Integral-Power, I see myself and everyone else around me as one unit. I experience the world from within that unit. I see my layers and those of the people around me.

Rising to pure potential, in my mind's eye, I am Infinite-Power. There are no more layers. I am with the source.

7

Quieting the Mind

The next morning Prince Pouchon woke when the rooster crowed. He went by the waterfall to find Savante sitting in silence. The young prince was intrigued. Since he had arrived at the easternmost village he noticed everyone who lived there spent time in silence; once in the morning and once in the evening. Some even practiced it during the course of the day.

"Why do you sit in silence, Savante?"

"It is called meditating. It is a way of quieting the mind."

"How does that benefit you?"

"When I silence my mind I open myself for suggestions from the divine. I create Infinite-Power. Great men and women have practiced this for centuries with amazing results."

"Can I practice meditating?"

"Anyone can meditate. It benefits everyone and it is very simple."

Prince Pouchon jotted down the directions as Savante dictated them to him.

Find a comfortable area where you will not be disturbed. Then follow these simple steps:

+ Shake your body out to help loosen it up.

+ Sit up comfortably in a chair with your back straight and your feet flat on the floor.

✦ Place your palms on your knees.

✦ Close your eyes.

✦ Breathe in deeply and slowly. Exhale slowly.

✦ Breathe in deeply and slowly again. Exhale slowly.

✦ Now breathe normally while focusing on the rise and fall of your chest.

✦ As you breathe in, imagine that you are receiving love and energy from the universe.

✦ As you exhale, imagine you are sharing that love and energy with every living creature in the universe. Feel yourself in a higher state.

✦ Remain in that state for five minutes.

✦ Then consciously feel your toes, then your knees, your hands, your gut, your heart, and your breathing.

✦ Breathe in deeply and slowly. Exhale slowly.

✦ Now slowly open your eyes.

"Go practice. Do it now," said Savante.

Prince Pouchon found a quiet spot, closed his eyes and focused on his breathing. Soon thoughts from the previous day filled his mind. He slipped to Self-Power. "I am confused. It seems only logical if everyone has the same potentiality, everyone should be successful." He made a mental note to talk to Savante about his thoughts and focused on his breathing again. Meditating was simple to practice.

8

As You Believe, So You Will Reap

That morning the young prince accompanied Savante on her usual walk around the village. She noticed he was in deep thought and did not intrude. Instead, she took him to visit an old friend, Richa. Prince Pouchon was not in a mood to visit anyone.

Richa was among the wealthiest men in the village. He had a huge castle and many servants. Prince Pouchon recognized and seized the opportunity to clarify his dilemma.

"Richa, why do you think some people are poor, while others are rich? Why is it some people have an easy life, while others seem to struggle throughout their entire existence without ever succeeding?"

"Well my young prince, I don't think anybody has an easy life. People express their potential in different ways."

"I'm not sure I'm following. I know we all share the same potential. So anything you can accomplish I can do just as well, according to my own abilities."

"That is correct, my young prince."

"Then how come you are rich while others are not?"

"What makes you believe I'm rich?"

"You have more material possessions than any other villager."

"That may be true, but accumulating material possessions does not make me rich. For me, living a balanced life is success," said Richa.

"Okay, so how come everyone is not living a balanced life, like you are?" said Pouchon sarcastically.

"Success, being rich, is different for each person. People choose how they express their potential. They decide whether to act based on spirit, Infinite-Power, or ego, Self-Power. The difference between success and failure lies in whether they take actions based on ego and therefore fears, or based on the spirit which is our true self."

"I'm confused," confessed the young prince.

"You see, my young prince, we all start with pure potential, Infinite-Power. The next layer is belief. Then comes the body followed by action. Are you with me so far?"

"I think so," said Pouchon confused.

"What Richa means," said Savante "is that your path is determined by the type of layer you choose."

"That's right," said Richa. "The very first set of layers that you put on is called belief. It, alone, directs your path in life."

"Let me understand this," said Prince Pouchon. "At the most basic level I am a spiritual being. I have the potential to become whoever I want to be."

"So far, so good," said Richa.

The prince continued. "Then I put on my first layer which is belief and that will decide the direction of my life."

"As you believe, so you will sow. As you sow, so you will reap," said Savante.

"So you see my young prince," said Richa, "who you become is a reflection of your beliefs."

"Do you mean to tell me people's beliefs cause them to be poor?" asked Prince Pouchon.

"I am saying that everything a person is, is a reflection of his beliefs," said Richa.

"Do you know what a belief is, Pouchon?" asked Savante.

"I guess that it is something you believe in."

"Actually," said Richa, "a belief is the mental acceptance of something as truth, without positive knowledge."

"So yes, what you believe about yourself and others, determines how you behave. Your behaviors establish your lot in life," said Savante.

Prince Pouchon seemed perplexed. A simple thing like belief could not have such an impact on a person's life.

"Let me illustrate by telling you the three farmers' story," said Richa. "This biblical story was told to me many moons ago by an old Wiseman."

A man, going on a journey, called his servants and entrusted his property to them. To one he gave five talents of money, to another two talents, and to another one talent, each according to his ability. Then he went on his journey.

The man who had received the five talents went at once and put his money to work and gained five more. So also, the one with the two talents gained two more. But the man who had received the one talent went off, dug a hole in the ground and hid his master's money.

After a long time, the master of those servants returned and settled accounts with them. The man who had received the five talents brought the other five. "Master," he said, "you entrusted me with five talents. See, I have gained five more."

His master replied, "Well done, good and faithful servant! You have been faithful with a few things; I will put you in charge of many things. Come and share your master's happiness!"

The man with the two talents also came. "Master," he said, "you entrusted me with two talents; see, I have gained two more."

His master replied, "Well done, good and faithful servant! You have been faithful with a few things; I will put you in charge of many things. Come and share your master's happiness!"

Then the man who had received the one talent came. "Master," he said, "I knew that you are a hard man, harvesting where you have not sown and gathering where you have not scattered seed. So I was afraid and went out and hid your talent in the ground. See, here is what belongs to you."

– Matthew 25:14-24

"What did that story mean to you?" asked Savante. "What did it teach you?"

Prince Pouchon paused for a moment. "The three servants all started with the same potential. They were each given a certain amount of money. The first one immediately invested his talents and made a healthy profit. The second one did the same and doubled his talents. The third one was so fearful he chose to do nothing. The choices they made were based on their beliefs. This determined the outcome they got."

"So as you see," said Richa "it is all about you."

"The way to awareness is through self-discovery. Self-discovery is about knowing my true self. Being true is about realizing my potential. My potential is Infinite-Power," thought the young prince.

He continued visiting around the village with Savante. The prince wanted to spend time quizzing Richa but he knew that the Wise One would not hear of it. She wanted to make sure he had a chance to experience everything the village had to offer.

9

Dying to Each Moment

The next morning Prince Pouchon woke before the rooster crowed. He went outside to find Savante by the waterfall meditating. He joined her in silence.

"Where shall we start today?" asked Savante coming out of her trance.

The young prince had so many questions he wanted to ask. He blurted them all at once.

"Easy," exclaimed Savante as they walked to the kitchen. "Let's take it one step at a time."

They sat down at the breakfast table and had tea.

"I need you to run an errand for me, Pouchon."

"Anything you need, Savante."

"Go to the third house on the fourth road. Tell them I sent you to pick up a package."

It would have been more productive to stay and have his questions answered but the young prince knew better than to question the Wise One. He did as Savante asked.

"Have you found awareness yet?"

Prince Pouchon recognized a familiar tiny voice. He smiled, got on one knee and the little princess got on his back.

"I learned many things yesterday. I am slowly putting them all together. I still have many questions." He paused for a moment. "You know, I just noticed. You are always in a good mood."

"Where did that comment come from?"

"Come to think of it, that's a common trait among all the villagers as well," continued Prince Pouchon.

"Well, I 'die to each moment.' I let go of every day."

"What do you mean?"

"It's simple really. Once a moment is gone, I let it be gone. No holding on to past hurts or resentments. I leave the experience behind and I take the lesson with me and move on," she said in a serious tone.

"What if there is no lesson?"

The little princess looked directly into the prince's eyes.

"There is always a lesson," she said sternly.

"Is it automatic for you to let the past go?"

"Yes, it is. You do it, too. Sometimes, we get stuck in Self-Power or Other-Power and carry negative emotions with us."

"So, how do I move on?"

"I can tell you what I do and you can see if it works for you."

"Yes, I'd like that," said the prince.

The little princess jumped off his back and landed on her two feet.

"Okay then, let me take you through the steps. Position yourself in Self-Power, think of a situation that happened in your past that you want to change, something that is still causing you pain and suffering now."

"Okay, I have one," said Pouchon.

"Now bring up a picture of that situation. Do you have it?" she asked patiently.

He hesitated. "Yes, I can see it."

"Good, now pay close attention to the image that you are seeing. Is it in color or black and white?"

Prince Pouchon looked like he was in a trance. He appeared to be searching for an answer.

"That's right, keep searching," said the little princess in a low and approving tone. "Now is the picture moving or is it still, is it bright or dark?"

"It is a motion picture, bright and full of color," he said taking rapid, short breaths.

"Is the picture close to your face or far away?"

The young prince leaned back. "Close, very close," he said, now breathing even heavier.

"Are you seeing things through your own eyes as you experienced them before, or are you looking at them as though you are an observer?"

"Through my own eyes, from Self-Power," he said panting.

"Now, I want you to make the picture black and white."

His breathing slowed down slightly. "Done," he said.

"Turn it into a still picture and look at it from Third-Power, as if you were a detached observer, like you have no interest in the outcome of the experience."

"Ok, got it." He breathed a sigh of relief.

"Now imagine looking at the still, black and white picture from above, Infinite-Power."

Prince Pouchon breathed a deep sigh of relief.

"That's right," continued the little princess in a low voice. "Raise high above the picture until you can't even make out what it is … now tell me, what do you see?"

"I see a black dot," said Prince Pouchon relieved.

"Have your feelings changed about the experience?"

"Yes they have. It does not seem significant anymore."

"Okay, now bring the picture back up. What kind of feeling do you experience?"

"I can't really hold the picture in front me. It does not make sense."

"And that's exactly how easy it is. I do this all the time with any experience that causes me hurt. It removes the emotion out of it," said the little princess.

"Is this how you stay happy?"

"Yes it is. When I say I 'die to each moment,' that's what I mean.

I remove the hurt and I keep the lesson. I let go."

They turned the corner to the fourth street and looked for the third house. There, on the balcony, was a brown package with Savante's name. Next to it was a note.

How to have a good day, every day:

✦ Write down five things that happened in your day today that you are proud of, that made you feel good about yourself; positive things, they can be big or small.

✦ Now close your eyes, relive each event. See, hear and feel each moment as you experienced it before. Enjoy!

✦ Repeat this exercise at the end of each day.

✦ Every morning relive the five happy experiences of the previous day and enjoy the feelings associated with them.

✦ Whenever you need to feel good, just bring up one of the happy pictures in your mind. It won't be long before your mind does this automatically and you will learn how to enjoy much happier days.

"Wow!" exclaimed the little princess. "Imagine that every morning you wake up and you are given the power to choose the type of day you want to have. What kind of day would you choose?"

Before Prince Pouchon could answer, the little princess continued.

"When you realize that you have the power to choose your circumstances, you will know how to have outstanding days."

Each day Pouchon searched for positive experiences that he relived at bedtime. At first he carried a small scroll with him and wrote down every little detail. He wrote about going to the beach, watching the sunset, meditating, seeing a butterfly, going on a walk and even eating his favorite dish. The young prince magnified every experience, big or small, that brought joy to his soul.

Pouchon thought back to his first visit to the enchanted side of his village. That was an experience that caused him pain and grief. He looked at the situation as if he were a detached observer. He made that picture black and white and pushed it as far away as he could. This enabled him to recall the experience without any negative emotions. The more Prince Pouchon practiced, the easier it became for him to have happy days. Soon he did not have to write down his positive experiences. They just followed him everywhere.

10

Self vs. Infinite-Self

Every Saturday evening a group of people gathered at a villager's house to eat griot (fried pork), drink and play dominos. One such evening, Prince Pouchon shared with a group of villagers what he discovered.

"I still wonder how belief can have such an impact on our life," he said.

"Well, you know that our beliefs come from our experiences and from what we are taught, right?" said a villager sitting next to the young prince.

"Yes, I read that in the book *Becoming Aware of your Inner Power*."

"Then you must also know that depending on what you believe, you will either act based on the *Self* which is ego or based on the *Infinite-Self* which is spirit."

"Ego, huh?" He thought back to his conversation with Richa the wealthy villager.

"Yes, ego leads to fear," said the villager.

"You are talking in codes."

"No, not in codes," said the villager. "Just like you, every person has an ego and a spirit. When you are completely de-layered, you are spirit, pure potential. You have Infinite-Power."

"So where does this 'ego' come into play?"

"Ego comes into existence when you are layered," said the villager gesturing with his hands.

"Exactly what is ego?"

"Ego is the part of you responsible for preserving the layers. Acting out of ego is being stuck in Self-Power."

"That does not necessarily sound bad," said Prince Pouchon, unimpressed.

"And it's not," answered the villager. "Ego is only concerned with the self. It sees itself as a distinct entity from the world and everyone in it."

"Rightly so. We are separate individuals."

"That's true, Pouchon, but also realize that although we are different on the outside we share a common consciousness. In spirit we are all the same. Didn't you learn about that?"

"Actually, I did. At the core we are all the same."

"Can you see now how ego can present a problem?" asked the villager.

The young prince looked up to his right trying to visualize it. "Not really," he said stroking his chin.

"Okay, you agree that at the core level we are all the same, we are one?"

"Yes, I do."

"And you agree that at the ego level we are separate, we are individuals?"

Prince Pouchon grew impatient. "Where are you going with this?"

"Okay, okay! Now answer me this, if we make decisions based on spirit, what kind of decisions are we going to make?"

"Well I would imagine decisions that would benefit the spirit."

"Right, and since we are one at the spirit level, who are those decisions going to benefit?"

"Oh, I got it. Everyone would benefit."

"Now ego-based decisions ..." started the villager.

"... will only benefit the individual," interrupted Prince Pouchon.

"And why is that?" asked the villager

"The ego will make decisions that are in its own best interest. And since we are separate at the ego level, an ego-based decision can only benefit the individual."

"Now, you're talking!" exclaimed the villager as he grabbed the young prince by both shoulders and shook him.

The other villagers laughed as Prince Pouchon smiled and looked around embarrassingly. "So when I act out of ego, I am in Self-Power, and my decisions are based solely on my point of view," said the young prince.

"Yeah!" shouted one of the other villagers in the group.

"In spirit, I am in Infinite-Power. My actions benefit everyone."

"Ain't that the truth" interrupted another villager.

A short astute-looking man, with a long pipe in his mouth, cleared his throat.

"Achoo!" a young villager pretended to sneeze. "Here goes another philosophy lecture," he said under his breath.

The short astute-looking man, with the long pipe, shot him a fiery look. Then he spoke in a deep and dignified tone.

"I, for one, believe that people stuck in Self-Power worry about the future because they fear they might have to face an old issue again and not be prepared to handle it. What they fail to realize is that no matter what the challenge or situation, they are indeed well equipped to handle it. They already went through it and have overcome it. People have the resources that they need to do just about anything they want to do. They just have to use them."

The short astute-looking man then told the group the story of "Backsliding Blues and his Mate Worryetta."

Backsliding Blues and Worryetta had a very static relationship. They were not doing much with their lives and they liked it that way. They were the two saddest people living in the village. Backsliding Blues loved telling stories about his past. His whole life was about either how great it used to be or how someone did him wrong. He grunted about missed opportunities. He wanted to bring back the "good old days."

Needless to say that not much was happening in his present life. He could not move on with his life because he held on to the things that happened in his past. Even the seemingly wonderful stories from his past brought him grief. He was so busy living in the past he was ruining his present life. He just kept backsliding to the past and that made him blue.

Worryetta on the other hand could not stop worrying about the future. She had wrinkles at the tender age of twenty-nine. Worryetta had a rough past. She was abused by someone she trusted and a few others took advantage of her. On the surface she didn't appear to have any conflicts. Though she didn't talk much about it, her past crippled her. She found it difficult to do anything for fear of what might happen.

One day they decided to seek advice from the village's old Wiseman. He told them simply "The past is gone, the future has not yet come, and the present, this moment, is all we have."

The Wiseman explained that everything they had done in the past had led them to this moment. What they do in this moment determines their future.

Backsliding Blues and Worryetta were very grateful for the words from the old Wiseman. Backsliding Blues realized there was no need to hold on to the past since he could not change it. He decided the best way to improve his life was to live in the moment.

Worryetta realized since the future is "not yet" she had the power to decide how it was going to turn out. She also decided she was going to live in the moment. Together they were awakened.

Prince Pouchon was in deep thought for a moment. Then suddenly he exclaimed, "In order to find awareness, I must be awakened. In order to be awakened I must go through self-discovery and learn to live in the moment. Going through self-discovery means I have to know the difference between ego and spirit.

"Spirit is true. Spirit is free. It is who I really am, immortal. It is energy and it is my soul."

"That's right!" said one villager.

"Self-Power is limiting. It is ego, fear and death. To live in the moment I must let go of yesterday and not worry about tomorrow," continued the young prince.

"You got it. Keep going," said another villager.

"I achieve this by forgiving. I must forgive myself for any mistakes I may have made in the past. To forgive, I must let go of the past."

"Almost there, what is the last thing you have to do, Pouchon?" asked a third villager.

"I must release those who may have done things that caused me hurt."

"That is the path to awareness," chanted the group in unison. "The challenge is to learn to apply it."

Just then Pouchon caught a silhouette of the little princess with the tiny voice.

The short astute-looking man with the long pipe said, "Often times we know what needs to be done. Doing it, indeed, may prove to be the challenge. Here are a couple of things you can do to get started."

Prince Pouchon leaned forward ready to learn.

"One key to awareness is learning to quiet the mind; to spend time in silence. The ego, as you know, is very busy at work all the time. It is working even when there is nothing to do. If there is no work the ego will create something to do. It creates stress mainly from negative past experiences and amplifies them to generate worries about the future.

The way to counter this is to give the mind some productive exercises to do, such as reading, writing and inventing."

"I do some of this already," thought Pouchon.

"The mind needs a regular vacation from its daily duties," continued the astute-looking villager. "This is simply done by enjoying silence regularly, during the course of the day. Silence can be achieved while sitting in a quiet room doing nothing and thinking about nothing in particular."

"By silence, do you mean meditation?" inquired Pouchon.

"Anything that will quiet the mind is considered meditation. I believe that you go for a walk on a daily basis with Savante, yes?"

"Yes, I do."

Every morning Prince Pouchon and Savante walked briskly and quietly around the village. Until now he thought it was only for exercise but he saw it might have another purpose, as well.

"What you may not know," continued the short astute-looking man with the long pipe "walking is not just a fun way to exercise but also a great way to meditate and experience silence."

"Yes, we often don't speak at all when we walk," said Pouchon.

"You know, it is an excellent opportunity to experience nature, especially during the early morning or late afternoon. Simply focus on your breathing while walking and you will experience great inner peace."

The short astute-looking man with the long pipe stood up. He crossed his hands behind his back and walked away, shoulders squared and chin in the air.

"So ends today's philosophy lesson," exclaimed a young villager.

Each morning Prince Pouchon meditated for at least fifteen minutes. Then he took a short walk around the village looking closely at his surroundings. He did this consistently, with persistence every day until it became a habit.

11

The Daily Mantra

On a warm breezy afternoon, Prince Pouchon joined Savante for a quiet moment in the garden.

"Why do you think people have such difficulty building and living their dreams?" he asked, breaking the silence.

"Obstacles; people are just afraid," said Savante, convincingly.

"What do you mean by obstacles?"

"A very old Wise One once told me 'obstacles are those fear-provoking experiences we have when we take our minds off of our goals.' Obstacles are the reasons that people give themselves to explain why they are not conquering their challenges and living their dreams."

"What if they are legitimate reasons?"

Lips pressed, eyes squinted, Savante spoke sternly, "Prince Pouchon, tell me five 'legitimate' reasons why you have not accomplished your goals."

He quickly rambled off what he viewed as his top five obstacles, proving his point.

"I fear change. I lack patience. I have trouble focusing. I don't have enough time. I have trouble saying no."

"Write them down," said Savante. "You will need them later."

One evening as he meditated, Prince Pouchon was eased out of his trance by a gentle presence. He opened his eyes to see the little princess, smiling warmly at him.

"Now that you have found awareness, I want you to do something that will help you remember to stay in the moment," she said softly. "Fill this out."

She handed a scroll to Pouchon.

"Keep it with you always and refer to it often throughout your day," she said.

Decide what type of day you want to have. Identify seven resources you need in order to have that day. Visualize yourself with those resources. See, hear and feel it happen.

Today is a /an _____ day!

I am _____

I am _____

I am _____

I am _____

I am _____

I am _____

I am _____

For in the end it is all about me.

This is your mantra. Say it every morning. Mean it. Believe it and it will come to pass.

"You know, you never told me your name," said Prince Pouchon.

"You know, you never asked. I am Princess Eveille (awaken)," she said, as she walked away.

Pouchon's Journal

Awareness is discovering my true potential. Every moment I experience, is stored in memory boxes and filed away in my brain. I gather information from my surroundings using the SAM model. My life experiences form my Personal Power Grid. I use this map to navigate through life.

I retrieve information from my map in the same manner I stored it, through the SAM model. My grid has five positions: Self-Power, Other-Power, Third-Power, Integral-Power, and Infinite-Power.

I use De-layering to remove layers imposed on me, by others and by my life experiences. When I am completely de-layered, I am one with the source. I am in the position of Infinite-Power.

My ultimate goal is to spend as much time as I can in the most powerful position on my Personal Power Grid, Infinite-Power. To be one with the source, I must practice meditation and spend time in silence.

I choose my life using my power grid. Reliving positive experiences from Self-Power allows me to rise to Infinite-Power.

As I believe, so I will sow. My beliefs determine my lot in life. When I believe I can, I will.

Ego is the equivalent of Self-Power. Spirit is Infinite-Power. Decisions made in Self-Power tend to be destructive. Choices derived from Infinite-Power are empowering.

I use my Personal Power Grid to let go of past hurts and live in the moment.

Each day brought new surprises and challenges and Pouchon lived successfully. He was awakened. He practiced meditating and living in the moment. Soon the young prince was "dying to each day," letting go of yesterday, living in the present and looking forward to tomorrow.

·"What a concept!" he thought, "yesterday, today and tomorrow, all right here, right now."

Prince Pouchon was acutely aware of his surroundings, his feelings, his moods, his thoughts and those of the people around him.

The young prince spent many days working on his mantra. "What kind of days do I want to have?" he asked himself. "What resources do I need, in order to have the kind of days I want?"

One morning after their usual walk, Prince Pouchon handed a scroll to Savante.

Today is an outstanding day!

I am aware

I am de-layered

I am Infinite-Power

I am true

I am free

I am forgiving

I am outstanding

For in the end, it is all about me!

"Travel west," said Savante, "seek and you will find understanding."

12

Seek First Understanding

By wisdom a house is built, and through understanding it is established.

– Proverbs 24:3

On the Path to Understanding

"You need any help?"

Engulfed in his planning, Prince Pouchon did not notice the traveler approach him.

"I didn't mean to frighten you. I was wondering if you needed guidance. You seem lost."

"I am on my way to the westernmost village and I just sat down to rest and plan my journey," said Pouchon.

"Well, I can show you the way there, if you'd like."

"Is it a long journey?"

"It doesn't have to be long. It's really all about you, my friend. Mind if I sit down?" The traveler dropped his bag on the ground and plopped down next to the young prince. He leaned against the maple tree.

"Where is your journey taking you?"

"Oh, my journey's taking me to my destination," said the traveler.

"What is your destination?"

"My destination is my journey, you see."

They talked for a while about the island, their families and how they came to meet each other.

"Since we're going the same way, we might as well continue together," said the traveler.

"That would be great! That is, if I am not intruding."

"No, not at all, I don't mind the company."

"Give me a few moments then we can leave."Prince Pouchon stared at his wooden notepad. Just a few more entries and his plans for the journey would be complete.

"What are you doing there?" interrupted the traveler.

"I am setting my goals for the next week. It helps me stay focused and organized."

"Well, what if something comes up?"

"I will adjust my plans accordingly. It is a simple process. Let me show you how to do it."

The traveler watched as Prince Pouchon wrote out his goals for the next few days. Then with guidance from the young prince, he planned his own journey.

The roads leading to the west were hard to navigate and sometimes dangerous. They had to travel through seven villages before they arrived at the far west. After considering several alternatives, they decided the shortest route was to travel due west.

Day and night the two men traveled, stopping long enough to eat and rest. The roads narrowed and were full of obstacles, as they walked through the region. The travel became treacherous.

Finally, after a few moons, the young prince and the traveler arrived at the seventh village. This was the last stop before the westernmost village.

"This is the end of our time together," said the traveler. "You'll have to proceed on your own."

The young prince was thankful the traveler was with him during part of his journey. "This is for you; use it to write down your goals."

The traveler took the notepad from the young prince and nodded in appreciation. "May I ask you a favor?"

"Certainly," said Pouchon.

"Well, you know, I noticed every morning and every night you'd spend time by yourself. I also heard you saying some words in the morning ..."

"It is my way of living in the moment."

The young prince showed the traveler how to meditate, how to write a mantra and how to practice everyday awareness just as he was taught at the easternmost village. Teaching the traveler reinforced Pouchon's own knowledge.

"I must go."

"Yes, you must," said the traveler. "I will tell Savante you are doing well."

Prince Pouchon's eyes widened. "You know Savante?"

"I am from the easternmost village."

"You will always be with me," said Pouchon.

"And you with me," said the traveler.

On the third evening of the seventh moon, Prince Pouchon was within a few kilometers of the westernmost village. Fatigue forced him to retire. He fell asleep under the starry night.

The next morning the young prince woke at daybreak. He meditated, quickly gathered his belongings and headed west. He followed the east-west path to the westernmost village.

Seven roads ran perpendicular to the east-west path, which led to a beach heavily populated with coconut trees. A short distance from shore, the ocean and the heavens merged into perfect harmony. It looked like the sky was within arm's reach.

Prince Pouchon gasped at the vastness of the ocean. He watched as the fishermen brought in their catch and prepared their nets for the next morning. One by one the fishermen left the beach. All, except the last fisherman. He brought in his catch and then he prepared to sail back to the deep sea.

"Where did everyone go?" said Pouchon to the last fisherman.

"To the market. They went to the market to sell their catch."

"Where are you going?"

"Back to sea. I'm headed back to sea to catch more fish," said the last fisherman proudly.

"Are the others coming back?"

"Coming back? No, when they sell their catch they'll go home, to spend time with their families."

"Then will they come back?"

The last fisherman smirked. "No, they won't come back. They're not that smart. They'll spend the rest of the day enjoying life."

Feigning ignorance Pouchon asked, "Why do you choose to go back to sea?"

"I go back to catch more fish, of course."

"Why do you need more fish?"

"I need more fish, so I can sell more."

"What will you do when you sell more?"

The last fisherman cocked his head. "I'll have more money, young man."

"And what will you do with more money?"

"Then I can fish less, spend more time with my family and enjoy my life," said the fisherman proudly. "Now do you see?"

"Not really. You spend more time fishing now, to sell more fish, to make more money, so you can spend time with your family and enjoy your life later?"

"Well, yeah …" started the last fisherman.

"In other words, when you are old and tired you will get to do what the other fishermen are doing now …"

"Yeah, but they don't have as much money as I do," interrupted the fisherman stubbornly.

"Why would they need it if they are already doing what they want to do?" persisted Prince Pouchon.

"Because …"

There was a long pause. The last fisherman looked at his net, and then turned to his catch. His eyes moved up, as if he were visualizing something. Then he looked down to his left, as if having a discussion with himself.

"I guess they don't," he finally said, in a barely audible tone.

The last fisherman folded his net and tucked it away for the next morning.

"I haven't seen you before," he said.

"I am looking for Understanding," said Pouchon.

"You say you're looking for Understanding? If that's the case, you need to go see the Wise One."

"Where do I find the Wise One?"

The last fisherman pointed. "He lives in the seventh castle on the seventh road. I have to go now. I must tell my wife the good news."

Prince Pouchon stared at the inscription hanging on the castle's door.

In all things seek understanding

This must be where the Wise One lives.

"Welcome, I've been expecting you." A young villager, not much older than the prince, showed two rows of perfect teeth and held the door open.

"I am looking for the Wise One," said the prince.

"Strange," said the young villager, "people normally come here looking for Understanding. I am Sagè (wise)."

Warmth filled the prince's cheeks. Sagè's smile grew wider. "Excellent, you are right on time for our mastermind meeting."

Sagè met regularly with the council of elders. They gathered at his castle on the fourth evening of every moon to discuss, among other things, the village, their lives and their aspirations.

"I propose that the fishermen remove their boats from the beach at night. They destroy the serenity of the beach," said the first elder.

"You suggest that the villagers remove their canoes at night to help keep the beach pleasant?" said second elder.

The first elder nodded.

"Don't you think this will inconvenience the fishermen?" asked the second elder.

"I suggest one of us ask the fishermen how they feel about it," said Sagè.

"Why do you repeat each others sentences?" interrupted the young prince.

"It is our way to make certain we understand each other," whispered Sagè. He put his right index finger on his lips and winked at Prince Pouchon.

As the elders spoke, they copied each other's tone of voice and body language. Prince Pouchon imitated them and this made him feel like he was part of the group.

Late in the evening the mastermind gathering came to an end. The young prince and the Wise One went to the garden while the servants prepared a room for the young visitor.

"You had some questions earlier?"

The prince noticed Sagè was copying his body posture.

"I heard you and the elders repeating each other's words," said Prince Pouchon, "then I noticed you copy each other's tone of voice and body posture when you speak to each other."

"You are very observant. Most people never pay attention to that."

"Is there a reason you do that?"

"Let me explain the principles of matching and mirroring. There is a certain art to proper communication. Great communicators use a combination of words, tone of voice and body language. You can learn to build rapport with someone by pacing, matching and mirroring."

Pouchon frowned, "What do you mean by rapport?"

"Rapport is when you connect with someone. It is a bond that leads to better understanding."

The frown on the prince's face grew thicker. "How do you build rapport with someone?"

"Through pacing, matching and mirroring," said Sagè.

"What is pacing, matching and mirroring?"

"It is rather simple," Sagè responded. "When I pace, or paraphrase, it is a simple way of making sure I understand what someone says to me. This helps me to build rapport with the person."

"Paraphrasing alone helps to build rapport?"

"During most conversations people often answer what they think the other person is saying without really listening.

"Most people only hear about 7%. They spend the rest of the conversation formulating their answer and reading body language."

Prince Pouchon smiled faintly.

"Hmm, I do that," he said.

"When I paraphrase, I simply repeat what I think the other person is saying to me using my own words. I look and I listen for clarification."

"What kind of clarification?"

"I will get the proper cue from the person. When I do, then I formulate and give my response," said Sagè.

"What do you mean by 'cue'?"

"The 'cue' normally comes in the form of body language or words. The other person will nod, say something or give me some kind of positive indication I am indeed on target."

"What happens if you misunderstood what was said?"

"In most cases, the other person will correct me. In that case, I listen attentively and I pace again until I receive the proper cue. Finally, I formulate and give my response," said Sagè.

"Is it necessary to paraphrase all the time?"

"No, as I practice I learn when to paraphrase and when not to paraphrase. I always paraphrase when I have doubts and anytime someone is giving me instructions."

"I should paraphrase whenever I'm in doubt and anytime I'm getting instructions," said Pouchon.

Sagè grinned. "Right," he said.

"Is it really that important to paraphrase?"

"Blue," said Sagè.

"Blue?" asked Prince Pouchon, perplexed.

"What was your first thought when I said 'blue'?"

"I saw an image of something blue. I saw the ocean."

"All I said was 'blue', how did you get water out of that?"

"When I heard 'blue' I immediately saw the ocean. Then I thought about the last time I was there and how much fun it was …"

"Well, well, so you went inside your mind and brought up an image from your past which was associated with blue. Did you also experience the feelings associated with the image?"

"Come to think of it, yes …" Pouchon had déjà vu.

"So the fact that I said blue made you feel good about yourself?"

"Yes," said Prince Pouchon amazed.

"This is exactly what happens when you are having a conversation. The person says something then you go inside your head to make images. Then you come back out and miss some of what was said," said Sagè.

Prince Pouchon eyes widened. His head shook up and down.

"Paraphrasing helps me to stay in the moment instead of making references to past experiences and not paying attention to what is said. When I am in the moment, I am attentive and that leads to under-standing."

"Let me show you to your room," said Sagè.

13

Build Rapport and Prosper

The sun was soft. The skies were clear. Young boys played soccer barefoot in the dirt. Sweat blurred the goalie's vision allowing the other team to score. The players roared and beat their hands on their chests.

"I yearn for those days," Sagè sighed.

"I never had them," grumbled Pouchon.

"Pity!"

"You are doing it again."

"I am doing what, again, Pouchon?"

"You are copying my tone and my body posture."

"I suppose you mean matching and mirroring," said Sagè.

"Yes. I spent the last few days practicing paraphrasing."

"Did you have a hard time at it?"

"It required some effort, but it was simple. Paraphrasing allowed me to build rapport."

"How did that feel, Pouchon?"

"I felt I did less guessing and more clarifying. The conversations had more meaning. But what is matching and mirroring?"

"Matching is copying one or more characteristics of someone's behavior. Mirroring is duplicating a person's physiology."

"What do you mean by physiology?"

"Physiology is the internal and external expressions of the body."

Puzzled, Prince Pouchon asked, "How do you mirror someone's internal expressions?"

"The only way possible. Whatever anyone is feeling inside is normally expressed on the outside. Can you genuinely laugh and be sad at the same time?"

Sagè scribbled on a wooden notepad and handed it to the prince. "Do not read it now," he instructed.

Prince Pouchon placed the notepad on the ground. "When should I read it?"

"In a moment, for now I want you to do exactly as I say," said Sagè.

"Okay, what do you want me to do?"

"Look at my facial expression then mirror it," said Sagè.

"Watch my breathing then duplicate it. Feel my muscle tone then match it. Copy my posture as closely as you can. Do it now."

Prince Pouchon examined Sagè's stance. He watched the slow rise and fall of the Wise One's chest. Pouchon noticed the slight frown, the squinting eyes and the unfocused gaze. The young prince squeezed Sagè's arm to determine his muscle tone.

After a few moments of examining Sagè, Prince Pouchon sat down next to him. Pouchon mirrored Sagè's posture. He rested his elbows on his knees. His left hand cupped the right hand. His left thumb overlapped his right and rested against his lips. Then he slowed down his breathing to match Sagè's. Finally he slightly frowned, tilted his head to the left, squinted and unfocused his gaze.

A feeling of confusion came over the young prince. For a moment he thought he saw images of someone giving him unclear messages. He had the sensation that he was deadlocked. Pouchon felt impending doom.

"What emotions are you experiencing?" asked Sagè.

"I feel lost and confused."

"Now, read the wooden notepad."

Confused and lost

"What just happened?" thought Pouchon. "How could I possibly have that experience just by mirroring Sagè's physiology?"

The experience was incredible. Prince Pouchon needed a moment to regain his composure.

Then he remembered what he learned in the easternmost village. *We all share the same potential. Our true self is spirit and we share the same consciousnesses.*

"When I mirror people's physiology or match their behavior I build better rapport with them," thought Pouchon.

For the next few days he paraphrased, matched and mirrored every-one he talked to. With practice, it became a habit and Prince Pouchon felt connected to his peers.

The moon formed a perfect sphere. The circle of light around it pushed away the dark clouds. One by one the stars fell, making way for the darkness. Just a few more seconds and the moon would lose its glow to the heavy darkness.

"I have to get out of this," thought Pouchon his chest pounding. "I must find my way out."

The young prince raced toward the last glimmer of moonlight. But, alas, it was closing faster than he could run there. A heavy hand on his shoulder weighed him down.

Suddenly a bright star ripped through the darkness.

"Pouchon …" said the loud voice.

He jerked back causing the villager's hand to fall off of his shoulder. Pouchon soared toward the moon. The stars shined. The moon glowed. The darkness scattered.

"Pouchon!" repeated the now comforting voice.

The villager stood up, nodded toward Sagè and walked away, head down.

"What were you doing?" said Sagè concerned.

Pouchon stared at the Wise One with a terrified look on his face. "There must be a better way," lamented the prince.

"If what you are doing does not bring you the result you desire, do something else."

"Enough with the lessons, Sagè." Prince Pouchon simultaneously closed his eyes, covered both ears with his hands and leaned forward between his knees.

Sagè sat next to the young prince. The Wise One rocked his torso back and forth to the tempo of Pouchon's breathing. They sat in silence under the moon.

"I apologize," said Pouchon.

"Every behavior has a positive intent," said Sagè.

"I was talking to the villager who was here earlier. As usual I matched his behavior and mirrored his physiology. Then I felt engulfed by darkness."

"You were talking to Triste (sadness). You experienced his emotions when you matched and mirrored him."

"That was an emotion that I did not care for," said Pouchon. "How can I build rapport with someone without taking on their emotions?"

"You want to learn how to match or mirror someone without taking on their emotions?"

Pouchon nodded. "Yes," he said eagerly.

"As you should know by now, when people focus on their obstacles they fall out of balance. They don't see the whole picture. You can build rapport with them by matching part of their behavior or mirroring a portion of their physiology."

"Hmm, how do I match or mirror only part of someone's physiology?"

"Did you notice me; how I looked when I sat down next to you earlier?"

The young prince looked up and to his left. "Yes, I did."

"I had rapport with you, didn't I?"

"You did," said Pouchon nodding.

"Yet I did not mirror your total posture?"

"No, you did not. How is it possible to build rapport like that?"

"I matched part of your behavior by acting upset and I mirrored one aspect of your physiology by sitting down."

"You can do that? You can mirror just one aspect of someone's physiology and build rapport with him?" exclaimed Pouchon.

"That's right. I mirror their body posture, their breathing or their facial expressions separately. That helps me to pace their physiology without experiencing their emotional state."

"By mirroring part of someone's physiology, I can establish rapport without taking on any emotions. Is that right?"

"That is exactly right," said Sagè.

The next morning Prince Pouchon walked to the beach to spend a few moments with nature. A young villager dejectedly leaned over a canoe inspecting it.

"Is everything alright?" asked the prince.

"No, not really, I seem to have a hole in my boat. I can't find it. Each time I go in the water it starts to sink. But I can't find the hole. I need to fish. I must fix this," said the young villager.

Prince Pouchon leaned over the canoe and inspected it. He mirrored part of the young villager's posture.

"There is the hole," he said.

"You found it. So it is a hole! Now, what am I going to do?"

They searched for a piece of bamboo and repaired the canoe.

The young prince smiled. "It does work," he thought. "By mirroring only part of the young villager's body posture, and not his entire physiology, I established rapport without experiencing his emotions."

14

Winners Never Struggle

L ate that afternoon, the young prince was in the garden bathing in the gentle caress of the sun.

"You listed your dreams and identified your obstacles while you were at the easternmost village. What have you done with that list?"

Prince Pouchon opened his eyes. Sagè stood next to the hammock staring down at him.

"What have you done with your list of obstacles?" he asked.

"I have it with me but I do not know what to do with it."

"Let me see it."

With one hand holding each side of the hammock, Prince Pouchon eased his left leg to the ground and carefully rolled off to his feet.

"Where are you going?" asked Sagè.

"To get my list."

"I thought you had it with you?"

"I do. It is inside the guestroom," said Pouchon.

"Say what you mean, mean what you say. Be thorough and specific when you speak. *I have it with me,* is not the same as *it's in the guestroom.*"

"I understand. The list is in the guestroom. I will go get it now."

"It's already late. We'll talk about it in the morning," said Sagè.

The young prince went to bed but sleep did not come. The balance he had achieved was slipping. The clarity that he experienced was fading. Something was amiss. He did not have a restful night.

The next morning after meditating and going on a walk, Prince Pouchon found a scroll on his cot.

Obstacles are the stories we tell ourselves to explain why we are not building and living our dreams.

Strugglers are people who are stuck out of balance. They use their obstacles to explain their failure to achieve their goals.

That evening, as it was the fourth day of the moon, the council of elders convened at Sagè's castle. The mastermind meeting started with the eldest villager asking everyone about their week. He opened a big book that he carried with him.

"Tell me something good," he said to each elder.

"I caught more fish this week than I've ever done before," said one elder.

"My grandson made me a new walking cane," said another.

"I mentored a new seeker this week," said yet another elder.

One by one the elders recounted their positive experiences from the previous week. They congratulated each other on their accomplishments.

"Any unwanted outcomes?" asked Sagè.

"Any unwanted outcomes?" echoed Pouchon impulsively.

The elders laughed. The young prince blushed.

"At least you're consistent," said an elder. "That's the second time you've blurted something out during our mastermind meeting."

They laughed again.

"Have you ever tried to do something and you got a different result than what you intended?" asked the shortest elder.

"Yes, many times," said Pouchon.

"Ah ha!" said the shortest elder, "that is an unwanted outcome."

"What do you do when you get an unwanted outcome?" asked another elder.

The young prince answered confidently, "I compare where I am, to where I want to be. I then retrace my steps to determine how I got where I am, I make the necessary adjustments and try a new plan."

The shortest elder smiled and nodded approvingly. "If what you are doing is not working, try something else," he said and winked at Sagè.

The elders presented their unwanted outcomes. Everyone offered suggestions for improvements.

After the gathering, the eldest villager put an arm around the prince's shoulder. He spoke slowly with a raspy voice. "Say, I couldn't help noticing that you are agonizing over something."

"I am just so lost on this whole issue of strugglers."

"So you're struggling with the 'struggler' issue, eh?" said the eldest villager squinting.

"I read that obstacles are the stories we tell ourselves to explain why we are not building and living our dreams."

"That's right, young prince. Strugglers are people who are stuck out of balance. They use their obstacles to explain their failure to achieve their goals."

"I have set many goals. Some I have achieved, others I have not. Yet I continue to seek. Does that make me a struggler?"

"So you set many goals. You achieved some of them and others you did not achieve. Yet you continue to seek," said the eldest villager.

Prince Pouchon nodded.

"What do you do that strugglers do not?"

The young prince shrugged his shoulders. "I set goals?"

"Many strugglers set goals."

"I achieved some of my goals?"

"Many strugglers achieved their goals."

Pouchon eyes widened. "Oh, I continue to seek."

"And what do you mean when you say that you continue to seek?"

"I mean that if I do one thing that does not work, I try something else.

I keep trying until I find something that works. I am persistent. I persevere."

"That's right," said the eldest villager. Strugglers don't persevere. They may have desires, they may set goals, but they are not persistent in pursuing their dreams. They give up."

"So strugglers are people who lack persistence?"

"No, not exactly. Some strugglers are persistent in certain aspect of their lives."

"How can that be?" asked Pouchon perplexed.

"Many strugglers are defeated before they attempt anything at all. Some make an attempt but lack perseverance. A few are successful in certain aspects of their lives but continue to struggle in other areas."

"That is confusing."

"You see, Pouchon, there are three main types of strugglers." The eldest villager gestured for three other elders to join him. "Say, do you mind telling Pouchon, here, about Depreciator?"

"I'll be much obliged," said the first elder. He spoke in a slow, deliberate and reflective tone.

"Depreciator was the typical 'underachiever'. While in kindergarten he auditioned for the lead role in the school play. For reasons beyond his control the role was given to another child.

"In high school he gathered enough courage to try out for the soccer team. He didn't make it. The first girl he invited for a date turned him down. Sometime during his last school year he decided to quit. School was not for him.

"He worked at the local farm while going back and forth to trade school. After years of trying, he received his marks in a trade that he did not really care for. He interviewed for a position but was rejected.

" 'You are not what we're looking for right now,' he was told, 'but we'll keep you in mind if anything comes up.'

"After years of loneliness, he met and married a girl. They had many children but Depreciator remained utterly unhappy. He bounced from one unfulfilling job to another. His life never amounted to his true potential. Depreciator spent all his time telling everyone how he put forth so much effort but never accomplished anything."

"Can you tell us what was really going on with Depreciator?" said the eldest villager to the first elder.

"Depreciator … well, I had a lot of potential," said the first elder.

"You are Depreciator?" said Pouchon surprised.

"I used to be. Let me explain. I was talented, witty and smart. Although I knew the vastness of my potential, I remained in self-doubt. I was out of balance and made Self-Power decisions. For that reason I did not try hard at anything.

"When I tried for the school play, I was offered a part that better suited my demeanor at the time. When I tried out for soccer I was offered another position which I turned down. The first girl I asked out rejected me. But the next one went out with me. In fact I dated extensively during my youth.

"After attending night school, I was accepted to the university but dropped out because I didn't think I belonged there. At the local farm I turned down many offers to advance. I succeeded in trade school, though I never studied. The position that I was rejected for was actually offered to me a few weeks later.

"I decided a long time ago that I was not good enough. To reinforce my belief, I made a very scary picture, in my mind, of what I was like: failing, afraid, lonely, poor and miserable. Every day I played this picture in my mind.

"When situations came up where I had a chance to better my life I brought up the picture. Soon it became normal for me to see that picture every time I thought of myself. Until I realized that I was truly a Master Achiever."

"Now, what about Perpetrator's story?" asked the eldest villager to the second elder.

"Perpetrator was your typical overachiever," said the second elder. "He decided early in life that he could do anything if he had the right motivation. When he was in kindergarten, he auditioned for a part in the school play and landed the lead role. In high school he was the team's captain.

"He went to the school dance with his dream girl. Sometime during his junior year he was accepted to five different colleges with full scholarships.

"He landed his dream job and ultimately opened his own company. Perpetrator married his college girlfriend and had two beautiful children.

"He was utterly unhappy and frequently broke his marriage vows. His life never amounted to what he envisioned as a little kid. Perpetrator thought that no one understood him. Yet he spent all his time telling everyone about his 'perfect life'."

"So what happened to Perpetrator?" asked Prince Pouchon.

The second elder looked straight into Pouchon's eyes and said in a strong voice, "I, too, had a lot of potential. I was talented, witty and smart. I knew the vastness of my potential but I felt undeserving of this gift. I questioned my self-worth.

"I was out of balance and made Self-Power decisions. When I tried out for the school play, I was offered the lead role only after threatening not to participate.

"I was captain of the football team. I never had a steady girlfriend. I preferred needy women. They gave me a goal to work toward. I had something to fix.

"I graduated college with the highest marks and became a top performer in my profession within a matter of months. Ultimately I opened my very own business and did well at first. Then when the business succeeded, I panicked and faltered. I recovered but never realized my full potential.

"I decided a long time ago that I was not good enough. To reinforce my belief, I made a scary picture in my mind of my self-worth, unwanted, undeserving and unworthy. Every day I brought this picture to mind.

"Every challenge I faced brought up the picture. That scared me into taking action. When my actions led to success, I again brought up the picture to remind myself that I didn't deserve to be successful.

"Then I started the process of self-sabotage. Soon it became a habit and I saw that picture every time I thought of myself succeeding.

"Continuously I sought approval from others for my actions all the while telling myself that other people's opinions didn't matter to me. Glory reassured me. Inevitably people came to expect great things from me. So the only way for me to get attention was through failure. I followed that path until I realized that I was truly a Master Executor."

The eldest villager gestured with his hands to the third elder. "Tell us about Exaggerator," he said.

"Exaggerator was your doomsday storyteller. If it were not for bad luck he would not have any luck at all. Listening to him you would think that he was bad luck personified. Nothing good happened to Exaggerator and nothing ever will. At least that is the way he saw it.

"When he was in kindergarten, he was asked to play the lead role in the school play. In high school he could easily be the football team's captain. He was the object of every girl's admiration. He was accepted to and attended college.

"After college he went from one job to another. Just as he straightened his act, something terrible happened. He seemed to have hit a string of bad luck.

"He finally got married but only to have someone to complain to. He was utterly unhappy. His life never amounted to what he'd envisioned as a little kid. He spent all his time telling everyone about his miseries."

"Let me guess, you were Exaggerator," said Pouchon.

"Actually no," said the eldest villager. "He wasn't. I had a lot of potential, was talented, witty and smart. Although aware of the vastness of my potential I remained in self-pity. I was out of balance and made decisions from Self-Power.

"For that reason I did not try hard at anything. I got the lead part in the school play and gave up after just one rehearsal. I never tried out for the football team. I never dated much because I thought no one liked me.

"I completed school, had some excellent work but never held a trade for long. The truth is I never found enjoyment in my work. Nothing was good enough for me.

"I had an amazing way of attracting good fortune and an even easier way of pushing it away. Chaos attracted me and I felt threatened by order. If there was no turmoil, I created it.

"I decided a long time ago that I was not good enough. To reinforce my belief, I created a chaotic representation of the world in my mind.

"I spent my time in that representation until I realized that I was truly a Master Implementer."

"Say, Prince Pouchon, did you notice anything similar about us?" asked the second elder.

"It sounds like you all had a similar story. Even the way you told the stories seemed the same. I felt as though you were all in the same predicament."

"So our stories were similar to you?" said the first elder.

The young prince nodded. "But I am confused though. How did you all change your lives?"

The eldest villager opened his big book. He licked the tip of his index and middle finger and flipped through a few pages. "Ah, read this!" he said.

Three men went to see an old Wise One. They wanted to find out how to succeed in life, as the old Wise One was known for helping even the most recalcitrant failures succeed. She has never failed. Not once.

When the three men arrived, they joined fifty other men already at the Wise One's shack waiting to see her. All the men waited for the Wise One to make her appearance but she never did. The men grew impatient. One by one they left.

On the seventh day, when the Wise One came out of her shack, only nine men remained. She stared at the men with disgust and said as loudly as she could, "Only three of you will follow the instructions that I'm about to give you and only one will succeed."

That does not make sense, the men thought. *Everyone who has ever been trained by the Wise One became a great success.*

"Do not waste my time," she continued, "if you are *aware* that you are the one, please stay. Everyone else leave now."

Three men quickly left.

"There are still six of you here. Do you *understand*? Only one will succeed. The others must leave now."

Three more men gathered their belongings and went away.

Taking time to stare each man in the eyes, she asked, "Do you *believe* that you are the one?"

The three men did not budge.

The Wise One went back inside her tent. She called each man inside separately and swore them to secrecy until they became successful. To each man she said, "There are three types of strugglers: the underachiever, the overachiever and the mid-performer.

The underachiever cannot do anything right. Everything in his life is a hassle. The underachiever has no meaningful relationships.

He gives up easily and loves to tell stories about his life's difficulties. There are no positive experiences in his life because he deletes them, while emphasizing the experiences that he views as negative. His goal is pity. He is motivated by the fear of failure, not measuring up.

When the underachiever is in balance he becomes like a Master Achiever. He is beautiful, gentle and colorful. Everything he touches turns into gold. Life is bliss. His relationships flourish. The Master Achiever emphasizes his positive experiences and learns from his unwanted outcomes. He is motivated by the desire to succeed.

The overachiever (or the "under-expector") seems to have it all. He appears to be self-confident and self-assured. A string of successes validates his air of superiority. The overachiever distorts everything. Many are those who admire him but most merely tolerate him. His goal is validation. He is motivated by the fear of success and not being able to keep up.

The overachiever, when in balance becomes a Master Executor. He continuously expects great things to happen. He is confident. The Master Executor sees things from Infinite-Power and strives to excel. He is motivated by success. He enjoys soaring above and beyond.

The mid-performer is the struggler who blames all his misfortunes on everyone else. Nothing goes right in his life and whoever is around at the time is at fault. He takes one negative outcome and applies it to every experience in his life. He generalizes everything. Good news is rare from him but the complaints are many. The mid-performer is ungrateful and skilled at self-sabotage. His goal is sympathy. He is motivated by the fear of rejection, not belonging.

When he manages to achieve balance, the mid-performer becomes a Master Implementer. He accepts responsibility for all his actions. He is organized and systematic. A Master Implementer looks for the best in everything and expects good news. He is thankful for his experiences. Peace and balance motivate him.

I believe *you* are the one. Go and be successful. Do it Now!

Prince Pouchon paused after reading the story. "So what happened next?" he asked.

"Well, each one of us believed that he was the one. So he acted on his belief and became the one," said the eldest villager.

"Was there a particular character that you identified with, Pouchon?" asked the second elder.

"I identified with Perpetrator or Master Executor ..."

"Are you Perpetrator or Master Executor?"

"I am definitely Master Executor. I am trying to soar. At one point, I was Perpetrator."

"Now, what else did you notice about us?" asked the eldest villager.

"The three of you had the same potential," said Prince Pouchon. "Maybe on a subconscious level you knew it as well. But, you allowed yourselves to believe otherwise."

"Why do you think we did that, young prince?" asked the eldest villager.

"Based on the story you all were out of balance. Your self-image was mainly ego-driven."

"Remember that," said the second elder. "No matter what the struggles, the end result is always the same. When you are a struggler you lose focus and stop growing. Your goals are not clear. You have trouble identifying your true desires."

The third elder joined in. "It's like you said, Pouchon, strugglers are stuck in Self-Power and Other-Power. Even when they make the right decision, they make it for the wrong reasons, which ultimately lead to destruction."

"It sounds like it all comes to what I believe about myself," said Prince Pouchon.

"That's right," said the eldest villager. "As you believe, so you will sow. As you sow, so you will reap."

"In other words," said Prince Pouchon, "my beliefs determine my actions and my actions determine my outcomes."

"Well put," said the eldest villager. "Our beliefs determine our success. When we believe, we are ready to move. We sacrifice everything for what we believe in, whether it is right or wrong."

As he thought about Depreciator, Perpetrator and Exaggerator, Prince Pouchon realized that strugglers have strong beliefs. People may be moving in the wrong direction and not even realize it because they are indeed strugglers, with self-limiting beliefs.

"What do I believe about myself?" he wondered.

15

Understanding Fear

The next morning, after fifteen minutes of meditation and a brisk walk on the beach, Prince Pouchon went to talk to Sagè. Before he had a chance to speak, Sagè handed him a wooden notepad.

Understanding Who You Are

You are back in school and your assignment is to describe yourself. The drawing above represents you as you are today. Tell me about who you are using the following four topics:

1. Spirituality
2. Love
3. Health
4. Wealth

Write on or around the picture. Draw on it if you need to.

Prince Pouchon wrote down his religious beliefs. He listed his capabilities. He wrote about his potential, his accomplishments and his health. Using colors he illustrated his size, his looks and even his body shape.

"What, if anything new, did you discover about yourself?" asked Sagè.

"I am not sure I found out anything new at all."

"Tell me about one item on the list."

"I wrote down that I exercise regularly."

"What does that say about you in terms of belief?"

"That I believe it is important to be healthy."

"What else did you write down?"

"That I am a motivated person."

"What do you do, what actions do you take that support that belief?" asked Sagè.

"Hmm, I procrastinate a lot," said Pouchon.

"So your action supports the fact that you are a procrastinator and not a motivated person?"

"Why did I write down a belief that my actions do not support?" asked Prince Pouchon perplexed.

"You are looking at yourself based on how you wish to be. You are not being true. Go back and redo the exercise and this time do it based on your actions and not according to what you wish to believe about yourself."

Prince Pouchon took his notepad and headed to the garden.

Belief	Action
I can do anything	I try harder
I am aware	I pay attention to detail
It is hard to achieve success	I procrastinate
You learn by teaching	I teach others
Silence is important	I meditate

This was a revealing exercise. Some of his beliefs caused him to struggle.

"I believe that I have the potential to accomplish anything. I also believe that making my dreams come true will be difficult. That is a self-limiting belief. It will lead to struggling," he thought. "I must change this belief."

It was getting late. Prince Pouchon decided to wait until the next day to engage Sagè in a discussion about changing beliefs and facing fears.

The next morning, the rooster crowed, Prince Pouchon ran to the garden. He searched the castle. He dashed to the waterfall. Alas, he did not find Sagè.

Anxious and excited the young prince did not realize that it was the fifth day; the day of morning fast and meditation.

Usually they met at the beach or by the waterfall where they spent the morning meditating. When he finally realized what day it was he went to join the Wise One at the beach.

"I apologize for my lateness," said Pouchon.

"The moment is as it should be. Why are you so agitated?"

"I realized yesterday that my actions are determined by my beliefs."

"Yes, we talked about that. 'As you believe so you will sow; as you sow …' "

"… so you will reap. I know. Sometimes I don't act according to my beliefs and it is because I am out of balance. It is not just a matter of not being true," said Pouchon.

"It's always about being true. It's always about you," said Sagè. "If you are out of balance it is because you are not being true. And of course, if you are not true then you are not free."

"I realize that I have a self-limiting belief that is causing me to be a struggler. I believe that accomplishing my goals is difficult. How do I change that belief?" asked Prince Pouchon.

"Begin by being honest. Write down your limiting beliefs. Match them to a type of struggler—Depreciator, Perpetrator or Exaggerator. That will make you aware of your beliefs and the struggles that you endure.

"Then write down the new beliefs that you want to have in the place of your limiting beliefs. Ask yourself, 'What actions do I have to take to match these new beliefs?' Picture your new beliefs in your mind. Make sure they shape into a colorful motion picture.

"Now see yourself taking the actions that are congruent with your new beliefs. Enjoy this feeling and remember it."

Prince Pouchon pulled out his wooden notepad and said with a smile on his face. "Do you mind repeating that?"

They both laughed and Sagè repeated the steps while Prince Pouchon carefully jotted them down.

- Begin by being honest.
- Write down your limiting beliefs.
- Match them to a type of struggler (Depreciator, Perpetrator or Exaggerator).
- Write down the new beliefs that you want to have in the place of your limiting beliefs.
- Ask yourself, "What actions do I have to take to match these new beliefs?"
- Picture your new beliefs in your mind. Make sure they shape into a colorful motion picture.
- Now see yourself taking the actions that are congruent with your new beliefs.
- Enjoy this feeling and remember it.

Evening was fast approaching as Sagè and the young prince strolled back toward the village.

"I heard from the villagers that you are an articulate storyteller," said Prince Pouchon. "Stories help me to better remember important lessons." Sagè smiled. He told the story of the poor man who would be king.

There once was a poor man who lived in the Caribbean Sea. He wanted to be a great man. He wanted to be wealthy. He wanted to be mighty. Alas, despite his best efforts the poor man couldn't achieve his dream of greatness. He was so sad and discouraged that he aimlessly crawled through life, like a man staggering through the night without a lantern.

Every once in a while there was a little excitement in his life but it did not last long. If only he would get the chance, he could soar like a Master Executor. If only other people would agree to help him, he could be great. The poor man watched as many great opportunities passed him by.

One day he decided to ask some of the richest men how to become rich. The first one replied, "You are as I am and I am as you are." The second man told him, "Discover your potential." The third one said, "Believe in your potential and express it through your actions."

The next morning, Pouchon went to the beach and observed as the fishermen brought in their catch from the deep sea. Some had ten baskets of fish. Others had twenty. Yet a few had fifty or more, each according to his needs. Crouched under a coconut tree, Prince Pouchon watched as the fishermen folded their nets and left to enjoy their life.

Suddenly, the young prince jumped to his feet and sprinted toward the village. He skipped through the castle, to the garden and found Sagè next to the waterfall.

"I figured it out! I got it!" said Pouchon.

"You figured what out?"

"Everyone shares the same sea of consciousness. We all have the same potential."

"That's right," said Sagè.

"We express our potential differently due to our beliefs. When I understand that my potential is infinite and believe in my potential, I express it in ways that lead to great success."

"How is it some people choose not to express their potential?"

"Fear," answered Prince Pouchon. "Fear is an ego-based emotion that I experience when I am out of balance and untrue. I act out of fear when I am trapped in Self-Power."

The young prince became pensive for a moment. "I act out of fear because I lack understanding of my potential. Either I do not know the vastness of my potential or I don't believe in it."

He pictured the last time he experienced fear.

"Fear is a feeling of anxiety over the outcome of something. Anxiety is spending today worrying about tomorrow. I worry when I am not living in the moment. To overcome fear, I must be true. I have to live in the moment and seek understanding."

He revised his mantra.

Today is an outstanding day!
I am aware
I am understanding
I am Infinite-Power
I am true
I am free
I am forgiving
I am outstanding
For in the end, it is all about me!

Prince Pouchon stayed a few more days with Sagè. On the last day of the season he decided it was time to leave.

"Head north. An interesting journey lies ahead of you," said Sagè. "Go and take responsibility."

Armed with the belief that all is possible and the understanding that fear is the real struggle, Prince Pouchon left the westernmost village in pursuit of responsibility.

16

The Perils of Responsibility

Personal responsibility is the springboard to action. A lack thereof is found in those who wither in self-pity.

– W. E. André

Navigating the Pitfalls of Responsibility

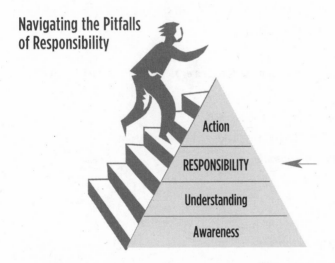

- Action
- RESPONSIBILITY
- Understanding
- Awareness

Halfway through his journey to the far north, the young prince arrived at a tiny village where there wasn't a Wise One. The villagers were going about their daily routine without any type of guidance.

Prince Pouchon was disturbed by what could be the youngsters' fate. He spent several moons in the village teaching young and old. Sharing the lessons helped him to anchor his learning. He taught from his journal.

Pouchon's Journal

Live in the moment.

The purpose of living in the moment is to be able to experience life to its fullest. I see more, I hear more and I feel more. Each moment is perfect and life becomes a pleasure.

To practice living in the moment I must:
+ let go of past hurt.
+ give up future worries.
+ practice silence.
+ associate daily with pleasant outcomes.
+ dissociate daily with unwanted outcomes.
+ enjoy nature.

I learned the difference between an egocentric state, which is based on fear and ultimately leads to spiritual death and a spirit-based state which is love and leads to being free.

I practiced goal setting by making a list of 101 dreams.

I identified my obstacles.

I became Aware.

During my stay at the westernmost village I learned:
+ how to paraphrase
+ how to build rapport
+ the three types of strugglers
+ self-understanding
+ identifying self-limiting belief
+ changing self-limiting belief
+ how to build a daily mantra
+ how to practice understanding

Every morning they gathered together for a brisk walk and they meditated in small groups. At the end of each day Prince Pouchon told stories about awareness, living in the moment, letting go of past hurts and understanding.

He stayed until the villagers were aware. One early morning Prince Pouchon decided to continue his journey north. The villagers accompanied him to their gate. They chanted in unison.

"Today is an outstanding day ..."

Prince Pouchon listened attentively to the mantra as tears streamed down his cheeks.

"They are going to be okay," he thought, as he walked away.

The northern mountain was the highest, most treacherous peak on the island. One look at it was enough to make the toughest islander turn back. Some considered the hike. Few attempted the climb. Hardly any made it to the top.

The northernmost village was situated atop that mountain.

Determined and motivated, Prince Pouchon visualized himself courageously navigating the pitfalls of the climb. The mountain got smaller and smaller. Step by step, hour after hour, one day at a time, Pouchon saw himself conquering the mountain.

The young prince stood on the mountain top and looked down. He was tired, yet he felt strong. Distant sounds from below came up to the village. Children played on the roads. Animals roamed about freely. A gentle breeze caressed Pouchon's face.

Except for a few stares, Prince Pouchon was largely ignored. Customarily on the island, people were courteous and friendly.

"This village must not get many visitors," he thought.

The young prince walked through the farms, passed the waterfall, to the market where the villagers bartered their goods. No one said a word to him. Prince Pouchon stopped in the village store.

A young man greeted him with a warm smile. "Welcome. It's a beautiful day, yes?"

"Indeed," said Prince Pouchon. "Can you tell me how to get to the Wise One's home?"

"Follow your heart and it will lead you there," the young man answered politely then disappeared to the back of the store.

"What kind of riddle is that? How does your heart lead you in the right direction?" thought Prince Pouchon.

Right then, he noticed a sign on the counter.

The buck stops here

Undeterred, the young prince wandered around the village. He found the village church and thought, "This must be a good place to seek guidance."

As Pouchon pushed the door open he saw a small sign.

Beyond this point your reasons are no longer valid

"There is really something strange about this village," he murmured to himself. Prince Pouchon tiptoed to the altar where an old man was busy setting up.

"Can you direct me to the Wise One's house?" he whispered.

"The answer is right in front of you. You only need to look a little closer." The old man turned away and went back to his work. As he left the church, Prince Pouchon got the distinct feeling that he was not going to get any help from the villagers finding the Wise One.

He felt a void in his gut. Heat rushed to his head. He was familiar with these sensations. To him, they were frustration and anger. "Why would someone, who can obviously help me, refuse to do so for no apparent reason?" Never had the young prince encountered such mean-hearted people. Normally things were there for him just for the asking. If the next person didn't tell him where the Wise One lived, he was going to explode.

Prince Pouchon did not know what to do. He decided to seek answers from yet another place. He proceeded to the village hall. There, again, he saw a sign as he entered the door.

It's all about you

Desperate and irritated, Pouchon uttered to himself, "It's not about me; it's all about finding the Wise One. I have questions that need answers and only the Wise One can answer them. I journeyed here from so far away and all I get are these signs; nobody wants to help."

He marched up to the counter where an older woman appeared to be busy working. She flashed him a big smile and purred, "I haven't seen you here before. You must be from another village. How are your travels going?"

Prince Pouchon struggled to keep his composure. "I have been here a few hours now, seeking directions to the Wise One's home. Everywhere I go, no one wants to help me."

His voice was pressured, his palms were sweaty and his pulse raced. He knew he was upset but he could not help himself. The experience was deeply frustrating.

"I visited other villages before and the villagers were not like the ones here," he said.

The older lady smiled at him comfortingly. She put an arm on his shoulder to reassure him.

"Most people who are new to the village have the same perception," she said. "Seek and you will find. Your journey will not be in vain." Then she walked away.

Prince Pouchon wanted to scream. She did not tell him how to find the Wise One either. He went outside and sat by the side of the road.

"Turning back is not an option. I must find the Wise One. I am utterly confused." Eyes closed, the young prince breathed deeply and slowly. "Today is an outstanding day ..." A few moments passed. He managed to finally calm himself down.

"What about all those signs?" thought Pouchon. He stared at all the castles. Each one was marked with the dweller's name and title.

"How did I miss that?" Pouchon chastised himself. "I will not complain, everything is as it should be, the moment is perfect."

With newfound confidence, he walked every street with a sense of purpose. Soon he discovered a beautiful little castle tucked in the far end of Responsibility Lane. There was a plaque on the wall.

Seek and you will find.
Follow your heart.
The answer is right in front of you.

Prince Pouchon was elated to find the Wise One. As he reached out his fist to knock, the door swung open.

"It took you a considerably shorter time to find me than your predecessors some are still out there ..."

"Looking in all the wrong places, I guess," interrupted Prince Pouchon.

"Right you are. I am Lepè, (old sage) and you are Pouchon aren't you?"

That was more of a statement than it was a question. Pouchon nodded politely.

The Wiseman gave the prince a small handbook, *"Navigating the Perils of Responsibility."*

Navigating the Perils of Responsibility

Every human experiences the world through sight, sound, smell, touch and taste. The events we experience are stored in a special section of the brain. They form our reality map. This map is developed from the time of birth until about age seven. We rely on this map to know how to respond to any situation we face.

Five-year-old Kenna loves the rain. "Don't go out in the rain," her mother says, "you'll get sick." Kenna plays in the rain with her clothes on. She develops the belief that rainfall makes her wet. This belief is reinforced each time she gets wet in the rain. One day she goes out in the rain and develops a cold. "Coincidence," she thinks. She sees no correlation between getting sick and being out in the rain.

Another time she goes out in the rain and becomes sick again. Going back to her reality map, she hears her mother's warning about playing in the rain. Then she realizes that the last time she was out in the rain she got sick. Lightning flashes inside her head. "Being out in the rain causes me to be sick." She develops a new belief about rain. She now avoids it.

Kenna realizes that when she is sick she is not able to go out and play. She has to stay in bed until she gets well. She likes to play. She values playing. Kenna becomes irritated at the fact that she cannot play and feels that rainfall takes away her ability to have fun. Kenna dislikes rain. She adds "feeling" to her belief. Since "having fun" is important to her, she decides to avoid rain.

As she grows up she realizes that she does not get sick each time she goes out in the rain. Another belief is formed, "Sometimes I get sick when I go out in the rain, and other times I don't."

Our everyday experiences determine what we believe about the world. Our reality map is composed of events that we experience.

Those experiences form our belief system. What we believe determines our values; those values mold our actions, our criteria.

When we face new situations, we refer to our map for guidance. If we have no point of reference, we modify our reality map to include the new learning. When new events challenge our beliefs, we modify our map to include these events or we label the new facts as unusual or accidental occurrences.

Our beliefs are made of philosophical learning and behavioral learning. Philosophical learning is the gathering and processing of information. The events that we experience form behavioral learning. Our beliefs are determined by what we see, hear, smell, taste or touch.

Kenna is now age twenty-nine. Her boyfriend accidentally pushes her in the river during playful teasing. She screams and shakes violently. Kenna's boyfriend stands still, his mouth wide open, his eyes bulging; he shrugs his shoulders and extends his arms. He does not realize that she is afraid he won't love her anymore.

After he pushed her in the river, she went inside her mind and checked her reality map. She hears her mother's warning about getting her clothes wet in the rain. She remembers getting sick when she went out in the rain with her clothes on. She sees herself sick, stuck and unable to go out and play. She can't have fun; her friends can't be around her. She feels unloved. When he pushed her in the river she felt unloved.

Each person creates his reality based on his past experiences. Behaviors are dictated by those experiences. How a person responds to each moment is determined by his reality map.

Every reality map is different. No two people have exactly the same reality map. That is true even when two people are put in the same situation. Actually, the event is the same for both. But each experiences it in a completely different way. That is why at a sumptuous gala filled with music and entertainment, one person dances the night away, while another slumps over at the corner table.

Every one uses their five senses to experience the world, yet how they use them differs. We use our reality to create love. Love here, is defined as togetherness, a sense of belonging, being one with the source. The source is where we experience peace. The way we experience our surroundings is called the Love Matrix.

We each have a Personal Love Matrix. It is the process we use to experience the feeling of love. The SAM model is composed of SAM^i and SAM^e. (i) is internal; (e) is external. Our past experiences form SAM^i. S stands for sight, A for auditory and M^i for feelings, emotions. Most of these experiences are collected from birth until the age of seven. We continually update or reaffirm our SAM^i.

What we see, hear, smell, taste and touch on a daily basis is called SAM^e. S is sight, A is auditory and M^e is smell, taste, touch and action. It is how we experience the world in the moment. SAM^e is how we gather information from our external environment.

Information from our environment (SAM^e)is compared to our internal reality map, (SAM^i). We then give meaning to the information and decide how to feel and respond.

SAM^e is the tool we use to gather information from our surroundings. SAM^i is the map we use to process that information.

There are six possible Personal Love Matrices:

SAM	SMA
AMS	ASM
MSA	MAS

"I love you, Pierre, why can't you see that?"

She's said it five times and Jeanne cannot see what Pierre does not feel.

"What do I have to do?" said Jeanne, frustrated, "walk you through it?"

"Actually, that would be great," answered Pierre excitedly.

Jeanne experiences the world through SMA. She likes to see, feel, and then hear. Pierre is MSA. He prefers to feel, see, and then hear. Because Jeanne is primarily visual she talks using visual words. Pierre understands better kinesthetically, through movement.

We create the world we live in based on past experiences (SAM^i) gathered for the most part from birth to age seven. We compare our daily life (SAM^e) to our internal reality map, give it meaning, decide how to feel and take actions based on those feelings.

17

What You See Is Never What You Get

Lepè spent several days orienting Prince Pouchon to the village and its customs. They rose with the morning sun, worked all day and retired with the sunset. They did this every day without fail.

Prince Pouchon thought about his initial experiences in the northernmost village. They differed from anywhere else he had been. Through meditation, he realized he was out of balance.

"Lepè, when I arrived at the village I thought people owed me something. I was accustomed to having things handed to me. I did not know how to find my way without someone directing me."

"The villagers were actually trying to help, but you did not see it. That was not the kind of help you were used to, was it?"

"No, it was not," said Pouchon. "I became critical of everybody. I formulated negative and unfair opinions about the villagers. I called them unfriendly and unwilling to help me, all because of my own narrow and limited mindset. I could not see, so I shifted blame to someone else."

Among the many signs in the village, one stood out. *It's all about you.* The young prince had heard this saying since he embarked on his journey, but never inquired about it.

"What exactly does the phrase '*It's all about you*' mean?"

"It simply means, you are in charge of all your experiences," said Lepè.

Prince Pouchon did not agree. He reasoned that plenty of circumstances were beyond his control.

"Control is an illusion like much of everything else in our world. Each one of us creates the world that he lives in. So ultimately we 'control' our world," said Lepè.

Life to the prince was about destiny. It was already written and there was not anything he or anyone else could do to change that. Prince Pouchon knew that he did not create his or anybody else's world. He knew that he did not control his world. He had to go through the motions and make the best of life.

Sensing the internal turmoil brewing inside the young prince, Lepè said, "How do you experience the world?"

"Through my senses; I see, I hear, I taste, I smell and I feel."

"Okay, great, now tell me what do you hear, see or feel when I say blue?"

A picture of the ocean flashed in Pouchon's mind. "When I heard you say blue, I saw the beach. I smelled the aroma of fresh coconut, tasted it and I felt relaxed."

"So I said blue and you went to the beach! You weren't actually at the beach, were you Pouchon?

"In my mind I was."

"Notice that I never said anything about a beach or coconut or relaxation. Yet you went inside your head and created this representation of a world where you were on the beach eating coconuts and relaxing."

"Does this mean that when we experience the world we go inside our heads and create images of another world?"

"Let me explain it to you," said Lepè. "Everyone has five senses …"

"Yes I know about the five senses," interrupted the young prince.

"Okay, when I talk to you, you use your sense of hearing to hear what I say. When you eat food you use your sense of smell and taste. When something rubs against your skin …"

"I use my sense of touch. I get it."

"Good. The five senses are Sight (seeing), Auditory (sound), and Movement (touch, smell and taste)."

"I read about that as well."

"We collect information about the world primarily through what we see (S), what we hear (A), and through what we touch, taste or smell (M). Touch, taste and smell are grouped together to form movement (M)."

"I understand," said Pouchon. "So we gather information through what we see, what we hear and what we touch, taste or smell. What we see is S, what we hear is A and what we touch, taste or smell is M," said Prince Pouchon.

"That's right Pouchon. This is known as the *SAM input model*. Are you with me so far?"

"Yes I am. I read about this in the handbook. But I thought it was just for relationships."

"This applies to everything in life. Once we gather this information, we take it inside our brain for processing.

"We compare the images, the sounds and the touches that we have gathered from our environment (SAM^e) to the ones we have stored in our mind from previous experiences (SAM^i). We give meaning to the SAM input and decide how to feel."

"It sounds like the feeling that we get is really based on the previous experiences and not what is happening at the time," said Pouchon.

"That's true in most cases. We create the world that we live in by creating images from the sight, auditory and kinesthetic input that we receive from the environment."

"But no two people experience the world in exactly the same way," said the young prince.

"That's right. Some people gather their input primarily through movement (touch, taste, smell or action). While others lean more toward auditory input. Most people however, gather input visually."

"Since we 'see' things differently, will we not tend to create different models or representations of the world?" asked Pouchon.

"Then you agree that we in fact create the world that we live in?"

"Well, I agree that I use past experiences to guide my life."

"Take for example a flushed feeling in the cheeks or redness in the face. It may be labeled as embarrassment or anger ..."

"... or it may be exhilaration and happiness," said Pouchon.

"Exactly!" said Lepè. "Screaming out loud in public may be perceived as a cry for help or madness. Yet it can be extreme joy. It all depends on who is interpreting the input and the previous experiences that person is comparing it to."

"So I experience the world based on images stored in my mind, my reality map," said Pouchon.

"Well, each one of us has a map that we use to navigate through life. This map is made of beliefs and of past experiences we have collected throughout our lives. This is SAM^i. The 'i' means internal. When we are presented with new external experiences (SAM^e), we filter them through our map in order to make sense of them."

"What do you mean by filter?"

"We'll talk about that later. For now, let me illustrate with a story," said Lepè.

"I love stories," said Pouchon.

A few moons ago, I was out walking around the village when a young man ran up to me huffing and puffing.

"What is the matter?" I asked him.

"I just saw the biggest snake I've ever seen in my short life and it's coming to get me!" he cried.

I took the young man by the hand and together we went looking for the big snake. A small grass snake laid on the ground. Sensing our presence, the snake recoiled and slithered away from us.

"Was that the big snake coming after you?" I asked.

"Yes," he said, "but it does not look so big now that you are with me."

In talking further to the young man, I found out that he had been told stories about giant "whooping" snakes that whipped many villagers who startled them. When the young man startled the grass snake it slithered away.

With the story as a reference point, the young man went inside his mind, created a giant whooping snake, scared himself and ran. If I did not come in contact with him he would have dashed to the village and told a story about how he encountered a giant whooping snake.

The story sounded familiar to Prince Pouchon. It spoke to him at a level only he understood. He saw images of the westernmost village as Lepè told the story. "It is all about me!" he thought.

"So what did you learn from that story?" asked Lepè.

Prince Pouchon was startled by the question. He was inside his mind making images. "I learned that it's all about me. I have choices. How I choose to exercise these choices is my prerogative."

"Okay, you know that choices have outcomes both wanted and unwanted. What if you don't get the desired outcome?"

Prince Pouchon thought for a moment. "I cannot shift responsibility to other people for choices that I make," he said. "I cannot 'control' all the input that I take in. How I process it, is always up to me. Only I create the world that I live in."

"Let's talk about SAM^e," said Lepè. "Can you hear the birds chirping?"

"Yes."

"Do you see the colorful flowers behind me?"

"Yes ..."

"Can you smell them?"

"Oh, I surely can," said Pouchon.

"Can you feel the wind's gentle caress against your face? How about the clothes against your skin?"

"Now that you mention it, yes. But I did not notice them before. I knew they were there but I did not pay attention to them."

"We are exposed to many experiences, many sensations, from our environment. We use filters to limit the amount of input that we actually take in."

"Why do we use 'filters'?" asked Pouchon.

"To make sense of the world. We use three main types of filters: Deletion, Distortion and Generalization. We delete, distort or generalize our experiences to make them fit our model of the world. We then use that filtered experience as our 'real' model of the world. This representation has nothing to do with reality. It is not a true picture of the world. It is a model of the world as we see, hear and feel it."

Lepè handed a wooden notepad to Prince Pouchon.

Paris in the the spring. A snake in the the grass.
A kick in the the rear.

"Take a closer look," said Lepè. "You read 'Paris in the spring' when in fact it says 'Paris in the <u>the</u> spring'. This is an example of deletion. We tend to delete portions of our experiences in order to make sense of the world."

"Wow," said Pouchon. "I really did not see the second 'the' in those sentences."

"You saw it alright. Your brain just deleted it."

"What about Distortion?"

"Distortion is the filter we use to inaccurately describe our experiences," said Lepè. "Remember the story about the young man and the snake?"

"Yes, he saw a small snake but said there was a giant whooping snake following him."

"That's right. He 'distorted' his experience. A small grass snake became a 'giant whooping snake'."

"So what about Generalization?" asked Pouchon. "Is that what I did when I arrived here?"

"I don't know. What did you do?"

"I expected everyone to be friendly. They were supposed to greet me and show me how to find your castle. When they did not, I felt disappointed, frustrated, angry and defeated. I felt that *all* the villagers were unhelpful even though I only had contact with a few."

Lepè smiled. "People generalize when they take one experience either good or bad, and apply it to a whole class of experiences."

"In my case, I took the fact that a few people did not want to help and generalized it to include everyone in the village."

"That's right," said Lepè.

"So filters are bad then? The villagers were helping. I distorted their actions based on my past experiences. Then, I generalized it to everyone. This is dangerous."

"Filters are neither good, nor bad. They are just tools we use to handle the large amount of stimuli we are exposed to on a daily basis. Can you imagine what it would be like if you did not filter out some of the input from the environment?"

"I would see everything, hear every sound and feel every touch. That is a lot to handle," said Pouchon.

"Indeed it would be. The key is to be aware of our filters and how we use them."

Prince Pouchon was intrigued by this. He never considered that he had the power to control the world that he lived in. Pouchon agreed he could limit the type and amount of stimuli that he was exposed to. That brought up another dilemma.

He accepted the fact he created his own world by manipulating information that he processed through his filters, his map of reality. But that meant that other people gathered SAM output from him, filtered it and created their own representation of him.

This representation may or may not have anything to do with what he actually meant to communicate. That did not sound right to the prince. There had to be a way to communicate exactly what he meant to someone else, without getting it deleted, distorted or generalized.

Just when he was about to ask, Lepè spoke, "Now as you can see there are a million ways you can use this knowledge. One of the best ways to ensure that you get your point across is to find out which representation system you use primarily to communicate with others and which primary representation system they use when communicating with you.

"As I said before, we gather information from our environment through the SAM^e pathways.

"The majority of people use visual/images (S) as their primary representational system. However, people may use S, A, M or a combination of two or three.

"The best way to ensure proper communication is through a process called pacing and leading."

"I actually learned a little bit about pacing," said Pouchon.

"Yes, I know," said Lepè. "Say for instance that Joe is having a conversation with Bill the farmer.

JOE: How are you today, Bill?
BILL: Things are MOVING smoothly, Joe.
JOE: That's great Bill, I can SENSE that.

"What representation system did Bill use?" asked Lepè.

"Movement. He used action and movement words."

"That is an example of matching representation system. Joe built instant rapport with Bill the farmer by speaking using moving words.

Now, if the conversation went like this:

JOE: How are you today, Bill?
BILL: I'm FEELING great, Joe.
JOE: Wonderful Bill, I can SEE that.

"There would be no rapport," said Lepè.

"Because Bill used moving words; and Joe answered with visual words," said Pouchon.

"That's exactly right. Pacing someone simply means to join him in his reality, his model of the world. In this situation a good way to build rapport is by pacing—by learning and speaking his language.

"It is simple to pace; listen as the person speaks and pay close attention to the verbs, adjectives and adverbs that he uses. That will help you determine his primary representation system.

"Once you know his primary representation system, speak to him using the same system; feed it back to him the same way he communicated it to you and you have instant rapport.

"Now you can lead him, take him where you want him to go without resistance, and get your point across with ease and confidence. To lead a person you must first enter his world. You do that by building rapport."

"Can you give me some more examples?" asked Prince Pouchon.

"I will do better," said Lepè. "Write a short essay describing your previous morning. Then put brackets around all the verbs, adjectives and adverbs."

The day [started] with me [jumping] out of bed at about five o'clock in the morning. I [wanted] to be up before the rooster [crowed]. That is important to me. It [makes] me [feel] like I [am] ahead of everybody. I [get] the [sense] that I [create] an advantage by [being] up earlier than most people.

I [walked] outside and [meditated] in the garden. I [visualized] my day. Then I [ate] breakfast with you. We [went] on a [walk] together. I [felt] [invigorated]. We [talked] for a while. You [showed] me [how] to [do] a few things. That [took] most of the morning. By the time I [had] a chance to [go] to the waterfall, it [was] already [past]midday.

Lepè handed Prince Pouchon a long scroll. On it was a list of examples of deletions, distortions and generalization. There was also a listing of sample words used in the representation systems.

SAMPLE SIGHT WORDS: Admire, appearance, bright, clarify, clarity, conceal, dark, display, examine, face, focus, foresee, gaze, glance, hazy, illusion, illustrate, imagine, look, notice, observe, outlook, perspective, picture, reveal, scene, see, stare, survey, vision, visualize.

SAMPLE AUDITORY WORDS: Accentuate, announce, argue, ask, attune, audible, call, cheer, complain, clear, cry, deaf, discuss, echo, explain, express, growl, harmonious, hear, inquire, insult, listen, loud, melody, monotonous, mute, nag, noise, proclaim, quiet, reply, ring, request, say, shout, sing, sound, talk, tell, tone, translate, vocal, yell.

SAMPLE MOVEMENT WORDS: Approach, advance, barter, beat, cold, contact, concrete, deliver, distance, expose, explode, feel, force, gentle, grab, handle, hard, heavy, hold, hug, hurt, irritate, jump, lance, move, open, pull, push, pressure, rough, rub, run, scrape, scratch, sensitive, skip, smooth, solid, suffer, tackle, tangible, tension, touch, warm, weigh.

"Use this to count how many sight, auditory and movement words you used in your essay."

Prince Pouchon counted the words. He had a strong tendency towards movement, followed by sight stimulation, then auditory.

"This is important to know," he said. "It will help me avoid imposing my reality on others."

"Keep this list handy. Read it often and let your unconscious mind commit it to memory so that you can better recognize representation systems when communicating with others.

"As you communicate, you will learn more and it is a good thing to learn, isn't it? And as you learn more you will better communicate because when you communicate, ah, then you commit all these things to memory," said Lepè.

That evening Prince Pouchon fell into a deep sleep. His brain had to make sense of all of this. He slept long and peacefully. He dreamed dreams and integrated all his experiences.

The next day, the peaceful smile on his face could only be described as splendid. He felt refreshed and invigorated.

Pouchon's Journal

I gather information from my surroundings, then take it inside my mind for processing. To make it fit my model of the world, which is based on my beliefs and my past experiences, I delete, distort or generalize that information.

Then, I create a picture in my mind, attach meaning to the picture and decide how to feel. The external experience does not determine my emotions. The meaning attached to the experience creates my feeling or state. Since I choose the meaning of my experiences, how or what I feel is also my choice.

External experiences must be processed carefully. Information conveyed to me is processed through my reality map and assigned meaning. It is not the communication, but the meaning I give it that determines my response.

When my model of communication is not getting my point across, I will try another mode of communicating.

If something I am doing or saying is not getting me the desired outcome, I will do or say something else. When it comes down to it, "the map is not the territory." It is a representation of the territory. The map is for guidance. The closer my map matches the territory the easier I navigate.

"It really is all about me!"

18

Man in the Mirror

Lepè told Prince Pouchon many stories about other seekers who came to him. Pouchon's favorite was the one about a handsome young man who grew up in what seemed to be the tiniest village in the world.

His parents were wealthy so he had everything he wanted. The handsome young man had his own personal maid and butler. He attended the best schools and was considered by all to be well educated, charming and outgoing. People always assumed he lived so well because he was born in a rich family.

Then one day, for no apparent reason, he decided to leave home for a larger village. It was incomprehensible to the villagers that a young man who had everything would just leave it all behind.

They tried to talk him out of leaving. The villagers told him horror stories of other people who left only to return poor and defeated. The handsome young man would not hear any of it. He had a plan and he was eager to put it to work.

A few years passed and no one heard about the handsome young man. He left the village amid much debate and almost everyone was expecting him to come back within a few months empty handed and poor.

Some said he probably failed, but he was too proud to come back home. Others believed he became highly successful and broke through the stereotype. He was never heard from again.

"So what happened to him?" asked Prince Pouchon. "I sense that he met with success."

"Right you are," said Lepè. "The secret to the young man's success was not that he was born wealthy. He left with absolutely nothing and became seven times more successful than he was before. And you know the surprising thing? The young man said the true gift he received from his parents was responsibility."

"What do you mean? How do you give the gift of responsibility?"

"Well when he was five years old and feeling very secure and entitled to his parents' wealth, they put him on a point system. He had to earn his keep. The more points he accumulated from reading, writing, good grades and good behavior, the more successful he became. By the time he was ten, he was earning enough points to have a maid and a butler."

"I never had to do that. My father provided everything for me," said Prince Pouchon.

"At the age of fourteen when the handsome young man again took things for granted his father gave him a mirror as a birthday present."

"A mirror!"

"It wasn't just any kind of mirror. This was a magic mirror. There were inscriptions written on it. On the top it read *Together we can make magic*. On the bottom it simply read *Look to me for love, motivation, awareness, understanding, and responsibility—man in the mirror*.

"Since that day, each time he felt sad and needed a familiar face, he looked in the mirror.

"When he was distressed and did not know what to do, he looked in the mirror.

"When he was discouraged and needed reassurance, he looked in the mirror.

"When he left the village he only took with him *the man in the mirror*."

"How can I gain the knowledge of responsibility?" asked Pouchon.

"Begin by learning the two rules of responsibility:

Rule #1   *It is all about you.*

Rule #2   *If you think it is not about you, refer to rule #1.*

"Then learn how to practice everyday responsibility."

"Exactly how do I practice everyday responsibility?" said Pouchon.

"Pick a situation where you think someone did you wrong."

"That would be when I arrived at the village and I thought the villagers did not want to help me find you."

"Ask yourself, what did you do that may have contributed to the situation?" said Lepè.

"I was looking for help in the way I experience the world. I did not pay attention. I was unaware."

"What could you have done to avoid the situation altogether?"

"I should have stayed in the moment. I could have asked for more explanation," said Pouchon.

"Have you accepted responsibility for your actions?"

"Yes, I have."

"Have you forgiven yourself?"

"Yes, I have."

"What could the villagers have done to avoid the situation?"

"They could have been more thorough and specific with their directions," said the young prince.

"Have you forgiven them?"

"Yes, I have, it's all about me."

"That is all there is to it," said Lepè. "This is how you practice everyday responsibility.

+ Pick a situation where you think someone clearly did you wrong.

+ Now ask yourself, "What did I do that may have contributed to this situation?"

✦ Then ask yourself, "What could I have done to avoid this
outcome altogether?"

✦ Accept responsibility.

✦ Forgive yourself.

✦ Forgive the other person.

✦ Move on.

Pouchon's Journal

When I find myself in a position where I feel I've been wronged, I
should first take a look in the mirror and ask myself, "What if anything
could I have done to avoid this outcome altogether?"

In most instances I will find something. When I do find it, I will
accept responsibility for being out of balance and forgive myself. I will
also forgive the person who I thought caused me harm.

In the rarest occasion that I do not identify anything that I could
have done differently to avoid the situation, I will refer to rule #1.

I will accept responsibility and forgive myself, I will forgive the other
person and I will move on.

19

It's All About You

One morning after his usual walk, Prince Pouchon was about to go mingle with the villagers when Lepè took him aside to talk about goals and dreams.

"During your journey you have learned about awareness and understanding. You identified your goals, determined your obstacles, figured out your struggles and discovered your beliefs. I want to know, what have you done so far to realize your goals?"

Prince Pouchon did not expect this kind of direct inquiry. He felt uncomfortable. He was stunned.

"Have you done anything at all?" Lepè persisted.

Regaining his composure, Prince Pouchon said, "When you asked me the question, I felt the need to justify myself to you. Then I realized that I don't have to. *It's all about me.* Are you asking because you want to help or are you asking just because you want to know?"

Lepè smiled and nodded.

"I'm asking because I want to know how far you are in your studies."

Prince Pouchon sensed that he was about to learn something new.

"I am coming along well with my studies. But I am not sure how to apply all the lessons."

"You are aware of your desires. You understand your struggles, now you have to accept responsibility. Do you remember the exercise that you did while learning understanding?"

"Which one? There were so many."

"The one pertaining to beliefs. I want you to list your beliefs as they relate to spirituality, love, health and wealth."

Lepè handed a small scroll to Pouchon.

"Follow the steps laid out here," he said. "Take as long as you need. This will help you accept responsibility."

Write down your beliefs as they really are and not as you wish them to be. Record at least five beliefs per topic.

 Spirituality

1. I believe in God
2. One consciousness
3. God is with me always
4. Pure Potential
5. Infinite wisdom

 Love

1. Love is good
2. Family comes first
3. Love is attentive
4. Love is giving
5. Love is selfless

 Health

1. Health is important
2. Proper nutrition
3. Movement
4. Involves body and mind
5. Promotes wealth

 Wealth

1. It is ok to be wealthy
2. Wealth is not happiness
3. Available to all
4. Money is not wealth
5. Money is volatile

Once you have completed this list, I want you to then write five actions that you take in each category.

 Spirituality

1. I pray
2. I try not to judge
3. I study God's ways
4. I meditate
5. I spend time in silence

 Love

1. I let go of the past
2. I forgive
3. I take care of loved ones
4. I give
5. Spend time with family

Health	Wealth
1. I fast	1. I plan
2. I eat right	2. I visualize wealth
3. I exercise	3. I work hard
4. I meditate	4. I share it
5. I read	5. I pay my debts in full

Prince Pouchon completed this task quickly since he had done the same thing at the westernmost village.

Pouchon's Journal

I compare my beliefs in each category to my actions. Are they congruent or incongruent? Does the action go well with the belief? If the beliefs are compatible with the actions, then I am on the right path. If the beliefs and the actions do not match, then I ask myself:

1. What does it mean to me to take X action?
2. How is taking X action a problem for me?
3. What other positive action can I replace X with?
4. How will this new action help me?

I must take ownership of my goals. The first step is to commit. When I commit to my aspirations, I am broadcasting my intentions. There is something very powerful about that. I am putting the universe on notice that I have made up my mind to do something. My body, my physiology responds by getting ready to perform any activity that is required to help me keep my commitment.

The divine responds by providing me the necessary tools to make my journey a smooth one.

That is the power of intention at work. This happens for a couple of reasons. I will find what I am looking for. When I make up my mind to do something I intuitively find my way. All I have to do is look, listen and feel from Infinite-Power. The answer is always with me.

Once I commit, the path to success will be revealed to me. When I find it, I must step up. "Stepping up" is taking responsibility. This is how I create my success.

Responsibility is to success, as oxygen is to the brain. It is like a fountain of fresh spring water. In its presence the flowers will bloom, the trees will grow taller and greener, even the villagers will glow.

Without water life dries up and the earth stops breathing. A lack of responsibility will flatten my aspirations quicker than I can think of them.

⸻

One morning Prince Pouchon woke feeling like he was no longer growing. He recognized that sensation. Once again, it was time for him to move on. He wrote a new mantra to remind him of all he learned.

Today is an outstanding day!
I am aware
I am understanding
I am responsible
I am true
I am free
I am forgiving
I am outstanding
For in the end, it is all about me!

Prince Pouchon bid adieu to Lepè who handed him something wrapped in an old piece of cloth.

"A little something to help you remember," murmured Lepè.

Prince Pouchon's face turned red. He felt a warm feeling rushing to his cheeks. His eyes narrowed and his pupils dilated. He could feel his heart beating faster; and his breathing felt shallow. This was a new experience for him. They smiled at each other knowingly and they parted ways.

20

Creating Unlimited Personal Power

All hard work brings a profit,
but mere talk leads only to poverty.

– Proverbs 13:23

Taking Right Action

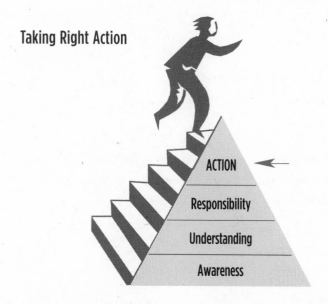

After he left the northernmost village he unwrapped the object Lepè gave him. It was an old magic mirror. Pouchon felt grateful for the gift.

He made good use of it. Lepè had told him the story about a magic mirror. But where did Lepè find that one? Just then he looked at the inscription on the mirror.

Together we can make magic

Pouchon knew practice makes perfect, so he summarized his experiences in an easily accessible pattern.

Pouchon's Journal

In the easternmost village I learned to live in the moment.

The purpose of living in the moment is to be able to experience life to its fullest. I see more, I hear more and I feel more. Each moment is perfect and life becomes a pleasure.

To practice living in the moment I must:

+ let go of past hurt
+ give up future worries
+ practice silence
+ associate daily with pleasant outcomes
+ dissociate daily with unwanted outcomes
+ enjoy nature

I learned the difference between an egocentric state, which is based on fear and ultimately leads to spiritual death and a spirit-based state which is love and leads to being free.

I practiced goal setting by making a list of 101 dreams.

I identified my obstacles.

I became Aware.

During my stay at the westernmost village I learned:

+ how to paraphrase
+ how to build rapport
+ the three types of strugglers
+ self-understanding
+ identifying self-limiting belief

✦ *changing self-limiting belief*
✦ *how to build a daily mantra*
✦ *how to practice understanding*

At the northernmost village, I discovered:
✦ *"the map is not the territory"*
✦ *how I experience the world*
✦ *how I create my reality through filters:*
  a. *Deletion*
  b. *Distortion*
  c. *Generalization*
✦ *how to pace and lead*
✦ *the man in the mirror*
✦ *how to practice everyday responsibility*
✦ *the two laws of responsibility*
✦ *how to take ownership of my dreams*
✦ *how to create a new mantra for responsibility*

———

On the way south, the young prince passed through the same small village that didn't have a Wise One.

"Today is an outstanding day, Prince Pouchon!" said a villager. "I'm on my way to the beach to spend some time with nature. Do you want to join me?"

"I would love to," said Pouchon. "It's quiet. Where is everybody?"

"It is quiet. Everybody's busy carrying out their plans. Some are at the farms, others are learning ... things have changed since the last time you were here."

"Oh, how is that?"

"You want to know how things have changed?"

Pouchon nodded.

"I better show you," said the villager.

He accompanied the prince around the tiny village. People greeted Prince Pouchon with gifts of love.

He witnessed the villagers meditating. He saw how they enjoyed nature, paraphrased, matched and mirrored each other. Their progress touched the prince.

"Are you going to teach us more?" inquired one villager.

"I can't stay long," said the prince. "We must start right away."

He spent several moons teaching young and old about awareness, living in the moment, letting go of past hurts, understanding, and responsibility. He stayed as long as it took to ensure the villagers learned how to navigate through the pitfalls of responsibility.

When it was time, the villagers accompanied Pouchon to their gate.

"Today is an outstanding day," said the prince.

"Every day is an outstanding day," said the villagers in unison.

After he left the tiny village, Pouchon went directly to the southernmost village. It was surrounded by water except for a thin strip of land connecting it to the mainland. The village literally became an island when the water level rose. It was nicknamed "the island that almost was."

When Pouchon arrived at sunrise, the women were carrying on with their chores. The children were busy playing or helping out. The men were hard at work. An idle body, no one could find. Everyone was busy.

The villagers moved with a sense of urgency. It seemed they had serious business to attend to. Lollygagging was not an option.

When the villagers spoke to each other they snapped their fingers at the end of their conversations. Pouchon figured this was a local ritual or salutation.

It hadn't taken Pouchon long to find their old Wise One, a tall and heavy man with a serious demeanor, named Travayè (worker).

"You're late!"

Travayè spoke to Pouchon as though he was chastising a child.

"I just got here a few moments ago and I came right over."

"Young man, explanations are useless in this village," he said in a most annoyed tone.

"Did I take long to get here?" thought the young prince. Images of his passage filled his mind.

"Are you with me, young man, or are you going to stay inside your head making images of the past?"

Pouchon thought about his mirror.

"When was I expected sir?" he asked calmly.

"Our day starts at sunrise and ends at sunset."

"Then we have not a minute more to waste. Let us get started," said Pouchon.

He joined Travayè and the other men. They worked until sunset.

Many moons passed. The schedule remained the same; work from sunrise to sunset, rest from dusk till dawn.

In the village, Travayè was counselor, teacher and life coach. He also spent time working in the farm like everyone else.

"You are a very powerful man," said Pouchon.

"What I do, doesn't show power. True power comes from within," said Travayè.

"Yes, I understand that. But how do I use that power?"

"You have to unlock your inner power."

"That's exactly my point," said the prince. "How do I do that?"

"There are five levels of power: Self-Power, Other-Power, Third-Power, Integral-Power and Infinite-Power."

"Yes I heard about them."

"Then you know Self-Power is the most limited. It's the power that you experience when you take actions based solely on your point of view."

"I got it," said Pouchon.

"Good, Other-Power is the power you display when you make decisions based on someone else's, point of view."

"Other-Power is using another person's point of view to make my decisions."

"That's right, Pouchon. Third-Power is when you make decisions from the point of view of a detached observer."

"In Third-Power, I take action from the point of view of an outsider looking in."

"Right, in Integral-Power, choices are made from a team player's point of view."

"So in Integral-Power, I act as part of a team."

"Exactly. Finally, in Infinite-Power, decisions are made from a universal point of view; it is an accumulation of all the other position in your Personal Power Grid."

"That means that in Infinite-Power I see the whole picture?"

"Right, at that level you are one with the source of all power."

"You mean that in Infinite-Power I am in spirit?"

"Right again, Pouchon!" Travayè looked at the sun. "We should prepare for the mastermind meeting."

The two men gathered ten chairs and arranged them in a circle on the back porch near the pond. Moments later the mastermind members started arriving.

Pouchon pulled a chair and sat in the background. He observed and listened but did not speak a word. The gathering ended after a couple of hours. A young servant came by the pond to help gather the chairs.

Travayè arranged three of the seats in a triangle.

"Sit next to me, Pouchon."

The Wiseman gestured the young servant to occupy the other seat.

"Pouchon, I know you're confused about the Personal Power Grid," said Travayè.

"My quietness gave me away?"

"I don't think I've ever heard you so quiet before."

All three men laughed.

"I want you to take notice of this conversation," said Travayè. "Tell me, what do you see?"

"I see the three of us sitting here having a conversation."

"Now, imagine that you are sitting where the servant is, what do you see?"

"I see two people talking and I'm observing," said Pouchon.

"Pretend that you are inside the castle and looking outside, what are you seeing?"

"Three people sitting in a triangle, two are talking while the other is observing."

"Envision yourself within the group," said Travayè.

"I'm not sure how to do that."

"While sitting here, I want you to see not just yourself, but the whole group as a unit."

"Okay, I'm seeing not just myself, but me within the group as a whole. It's like I am a seed inside an orange but I see the entire orange from within."

"Excellent. Now float above, what do you see?"

"You want me to float?" said Pouchon, confused.

"No," Travayè grinned shaking his head. "I want you to pretend that you are floating above all three of us, what do you see?"

"I see three people sitting in a triangle, two are talking, one is observing. I see the orange from outside but I also see the seeds inside as well. I see the whole picture."

"How do you see all of this, if you are floating above?"

"By the time I reach Infinite-Power I have accumulated knowledge from all the other positions on my grid. I started in Self-Power, then I shifted to Other-Power, Third-Power, Integral-Power and finally I rose to Infinite-Power."

Pouchon thought for a moment. "In that position, a combination of all points of view is available to me. I see all. I am omniscient."

They gathered the chairs and went inside the castle. Pouchon was amazed he could change his point of view just by pretending to be in a different position. "But what does that have to do with the Personal Power Grid?" he thought.

"You must be wondering how that little exercise can help you build power?" said Travayè.

"Actually, yes."

"When you were sitting in the chair looking at things from your own eyes, you were in Self-Power. When you pretended to be the servant, you were …"

"In Other-Power," interrupted Pouchon. "Then when I was inside the castle looking out, I was in Third-Power. When I imagined that I was a seed inside an orange, I was in Integral-Power. I saw the whole unit from within. Then when I floated …"

"You didn't actually float, did you?" said Travayè jokingly.

"Ha! Ha! Ha!" Pouchon pretended to laugh. "When I imagined floating above the unit, I was in Infinite-Power, I saw things from each point of view."

"Quite perceptive! Suppose you have to make a decision. Where on your power grid would you rather be when you decide?"

"Infinite-Power! No questions!"

"Why is that?"

"Simple," said the prince, "in Self-Power I have only my point of view. In Other-Power I have just someone else's point of view. In Third-Power, I have the point of view of a detached observer. When in Integral-

Power I have my point of view, as part of a unit. I think and act as a team member."

Pouchon paused. "But in Infinite-Power, I am above the experience and have accumulated knowledge from all the other positions. I see all points of view and I am with the source."

"Why is it important to be with the source, Pouchon?"

"Any decision I make will benefit not just me or another person or group; a choice made in Infinite-Power will benefit everyone. It is a spiritual selection."

"Do you see how you create more power as you switch position on your Personal Power Grid?"

"Yes I do. The higher I climb the more choices I create. I have more viewpoints to work with. I see the whole picture."

"It's getting late, sir," said the young servant, "but before I leave, the farmers wanted to know if you were going to help them resolve their disagreement?"

"I will be there at daybreak," said Travayè.

The young servant left, leaving the two men in the room.

"I see so many ways to use the Personal Power Grid …"

"Yes I know," interrupted Travayè, "we'll talk more about it another time. I must retire."

The Wiseman patted the prince on the shoulder and left the room. Pouchon walked outside by the pond. He sat in silence then went inside to sleep.

The Personal Power Grid dominated the prince's thought. Over the next few days, Travayè didn't speak further about it. But he frequently instructed Pouchon to shift power position. "What power level are you in right now?" he would ask. He made sure that the prince was aware of his position on the power grid at all time.

One day, at sunset, Travaye handed a small booklet to Pouchon.

Creating Unlimited Personal Power

Personal power is the ability to remain constant regardless of the circumstances. This is an inner calmness not to be confused with complacency. A person who is constantly in Infinite-Power masters his destiny.

Using the Personal Power Grid can create unlimited personal power. This system, when applied correctly, can lead to great success in every aspect of life.

Emphasizing positive emotions derived from past experiences is empowering. Dwelling on negative emotions derived from past experiences is defeating. To grow, let go of negative emotions and emphasize those that create power. Infinite-Power is the most powerful position on the Personal Power Grid.

The goal is to remain in Infinite-Power as often as possible. The only obstacle standing between a man and his dreams is fear. This fear stems from dwelling on negative past experiences. To be successful, to create unlimited personal power, release the fear by letting go of past hurts.

The first step in creating unlimited personal power is to apply the Rule of Thirty. This rule states a person has thirty seconds, thirty minutes, thirty hours or thirty days to grieve any painful event.

One cannot, not live in the past. Recall that past experiences are stored in the brain and they serve as a blueprint for life. The key is to minimize the negative past experiences while emphasizing the positives.

The most easily accessible past experiences are those stored in the *self-preservation box.* This box is accessed daily for things like how to get dressed, eat, and shower. Also stored in the box are the negative past experiences that create fear. This fear keeps us away from danger, but it is often debilitating.

Since daily events trigger past experiences, whether to assign thirty seconds or thirty minutes to an upsetting event depends on the individual and the hurtful experience triggered by the daily event. As a general rule, a simple hurt that will not matter an hour from now, should be assigned thirty seconds. Loss of a meaningful relationship either by a permanent separation or death can be assigned thirty days.

A person should use his own judgment. A thirty-second problem to one person may be a thirty-day issue to someone else. It all depends on the person and how painful the past experience is to that person.

Once a time frame has been assigned, it is time to move to the Personal Power Grid. What experience was triggered? Relive the experience from Self-Power. Then move to Other-Power, Third-Power, Integral-Power and finally be one with the source in Infinite-Power.

In many instances some people will reach Infinite-Power quicker than expected. The Rule of Thirty implies that no past hurt should be held for more than thirty days. Once taken to Infinite-Power the experience remains, but the hurt is gone.

The Rule of Thirty and the Personal Power Grid should be used on a daily basis to create personal power. When dealing with family, friends, co-workers, relationships, past or new experiences, one can use this system to remain constant and powerful. Power is created by consistently shifting position on the grid to ensure understanding.

21

Transform Fear to Power

Pouchon read the handbook Travayè gave him three times over. Though it made perfect sense to him, he needed to discuss it with the Wiseman. The prince found Travayè at the village center coaching a villager and his wife.

"Think of the unresolved disagreement that you had with your wife," said Travayè to the villager.

"Um, Okay"

"Relive the disagreement from Self-Power. I want you to see, hear and feel the experience as though it is happening now ..."

The villager winced.

"What feelings are you experiencing?"

"I'm in shock," said the villager.

"Switch to Other-Power. Relive the experience from your wife's point of view. See what she sees ... what does she see?"

"An irritated and hostile husband."

"Now, hear what she hears ... what does she hear?"

"Nothing ... the husband is not saying anything."

"Seeing and hearing from your wife's point of view, what feelings are you experiencing?"

"Anger and frustration," said the villager.

"Go to Third-Power; witness the experience as a detached observer."

"I see and hear two people having a disagreement. But I feel nothing."

"Move to Integral-Power," said Travayè. "Relive the experience as though you are part of a unit, seeking a specific desired outcome. What are you feeling?"

"I want to do what's best for the marriage."

"Now, shift to Infinite-Power, and imagine rising above the situation. Rise as high as you can. What do you see?"

"I remember what I saw from the other positions; from here I see two dots," said the villager.

"What meaning does the disagreement have from Infinite-Power?"

"Unimportant. It doesn't matter."

"Tell me, what happens when you float higher?" asked Travayè.

"I can't see anything. The picture is gone. I can't hear anything. The sound is gone …"

"How do you feel about the situation now?"

The villager looked up to his left, trying to visualize his disagreement with his wife. His eyes moved down to his left. "I don't feel anything," he said. "There is nothing for me to feel anything about. The situation is gone."

"Now, go home and work out your problems," instructed the Wiseman.

The villager and his wife thanked the Wiseman and left him with the prince.

"Is that the only way to use the Personal Power Grid?" inquired Pouchon.

"The grid has many uses. It can and should be used in every aspect of life. During a conversation you can go to Other-Power to see someone else's point of view. At work or at play, you can go to Integral-Power to be a powerful team player. But the Personal Power Grid's main purpose is to create Infinite-Power; in that position, you are all powerful."

"I can also use the grid to release fear," said Pouchon.

"That's right. But how do you experience fear?"

"What do you mean?"

"Can you think of a time when you were fearful of something?"

"Yes, I can."

"Relive the experience, what was it like to be fearful?"

"I felt a void in my stomach. It felt as though something dropped out of me. My heart pounded in my chest, my pulse raced and my breathing accelerated. I felt ready to take action."

"Can you remember the last time you were excited about something?" asked Travayè.

"Yes, I felt …" there was a long pause. "I felt a void in my stomach, my heart pounded, my pulse raced and my breathing accelerated. I was ready to leap into action."

"You just described the same thing twice. Yet you call one 'fear' and the other 'excitement'. How did you know the difference between the two?"

"Well, when I experienced fear I wanted to run away. But when I thought I was excited I wanted to move forward," said Pouchon.

"You experienced the same sensations but you gave them different meaning?"

"When I compared the experience to my map of reality, it signaled danger. So I moved away. That is fear. The other event indicated pleasure. I moved forward. That is excitement."

"Then you're telling me the only difference between fear and excitement is …"

"Meaning," interrupted the prince. "It's the meaning that I give to the event based on my past experiences."

"If that's true, then you can turn fear into excitement," said Travayè.

"Yes, I can turn any fearful situation into excitement, simply by changing the meaning of the experience. I just choose to make the event a signal to be excited."

Pouchon's Journal

The Personal Power Grid is one of the most powerful techniques I have learned on my journey. I can apply it to every aspect of my life. It is simple, easy and it works well.

There are five power positions on the grid: Self-Power — seeing from my own point of view; Other-Power — seeing from someone else's point of view; Third-Power — seeing from the point of view of a detached observer; Integral-Power — seeing the unit as a whole; and Infinite-Power — being one with the source.

I can use this knowledge to create personal infinite power.

I make better choices using my Personal Power Grid. I work from several points of view. In the end I make decisions with infinite power.

22

Begin with Truth, Grow Free

Though he was a man of few words, Travayè taught by story telling. He had an unusual style. He started a story and asked someone else to finish it; this was his way of evaluating understanding of the tale.

One story was about a girl, Truth.

Truth was pure and simple. Nothing really bothered her. She was reliable, not dull or boring. She was stable. Despite all her great qualities the young girl had great difficulties finding and keeping a mate. Truth was desired by all, tolerated by most and feared by many. She had suitors but alas, her relationships were rocky.

Truth's personal relationships had that "on-again off-again" quality to them. People joked that she was "yo-yo" dating. She was with Exaggerator, Depreciator and Perpetrator, but none loved Truth enough to stay with her. They avoided her and deserted her for no apparent reason.

The first relationship was with Exaggerator, a surly kind of fellow who knew everything about everything. He was comfortable where he was in life and didn't like change. Exaggerator felt at ease with people who shared his views and had no tolerance for those with contrary opinions. There was no room in his thinking for alternate possibilities.

Truth's relationship with him was rocky from the start. She always seemed to say things that irritated him. Exaggerator eventually decided that Truth was confrontational and against him because she disagreed with him. He ended the relationship.

Soon after that, a young man, Depreciator, came knocking at her door. He was especially taken by Truth's beauty and her stability. He complimented her simplicity and class. Truth's relationship with Depreciator was also doomed from the start.

Depreciator spent all his time in the past; always reminiscing about what could have, would have, and should have been. It seemed that Depreciator's best times were behind him. He had nothing to look forward to. When Truth tried to help him see otherwise, he became annoyed and left the relationship.

Then Perpetrator, a handsome suitor, courted Truth. On the surface they looked like a match made in heaven. Perpetrator was handsome, outgoing, independent, and adventurous. He focused all his attention on Truth and gave her all she wanted, except of course what she desired most. Perpetrator had this way of doing things. He was great at giving. He loved to make her happy but he couldn't accept her love. He felt guilty and undeserving.

Strangely enough, Perpetrator grew irritated if Truth did not attempt to return a favor. Even though he would not accept her gifts, he wanted her to make the offer. Their relationship did not last. It seemed Truth was destined to lead a lonely existence.

As Pouchon listened to Travayè tell the story he thought about what a lonely life Truth had. The Wiseman did not tell the story for entertainment alone. There was a lesson. Though he was tempted to ask about the story's ending, the prince knew the lesson was his to find.

Travayè spoke specifically about Exaggerator, Perpetrator and Depreciator.

"I've heard about them before," thought Pouchon. "They were the three strugglers. Was Travayè talking about them specifically or metaphorically? Maybe if I compare these three men and evaluate their personality traits I can see what they have in common. Perhaps, there is a pattern that they all follow that explains their behavior."

"I've got it," exclaimed Pouchon. "Exaggerator, Perpetrator and Depreciator all had the same issue. They could not face Truth. Something about her made them feel uncomfortable and unwilling to walk with her.

"Due to Truth's free-spirited nature, Exaggerator felt constantly threatened and insecure; their relationship withered.

"Depreciator could not face Truth because that required him to give up his insecurities, let go of his past hurts and live in the present.

"Perpetrator thought he was not good enough. He felt unworthy of Truth's love and ultimately destroyed their relationship."

Pouchon knew Travayè might ask him to complete the story. So with these insights he decided to come up with his own version of how the story ended.

That evening during the rest period after supper, Pouchon told his story to Travayè.

Truth dutifully went about her days and remained positive and outgoing. She seemed destined to live a life of solitude.

One day Truth met a man she knew was going to be her life-long companion. He walked with an air of confidence. He seemed always to be expecting something great to happen at any moment. He was quiet yet assertive, and sure. He had an aura that made her want to be around him all the time. This man's name was Freedom.

Truth saw him as the handsomest person ever to walk the earth. It was strange though, people responded to him either with admiration and love or with envy and jealousy.

When Truth met Freedom they both felt as if they had known each other all their lives. It was a match made by the gods. They barely had to speak to each other. They knew. It seemed amazing that they existed so long without each other. It wasn't long before they were married.

Truth and Freedom enjoyed a mutually rewarding relationship. They understood the reciprocating nature of their union. They lived by a simple motto:

"Truth shall set you free. Freedom will keep you true."

"This is a good story," said Travayè. "Is there more to it?"

"I know the story doesn't end here, but I am not sure what happens next. One thing is certain, Truth and Freedom will make beautiful things happen," said Pouchon.

Travayè was pleased with Pouchon's insight. Night was approaching and work started at dawn. They parted company and went to rest.

Pouchon was thinking a lot about Truth and Freedom and imagining different ways their lives may have turned out. "*If I want ever to be free, I must be true,*" he thought. The young prince was so excited, he barely slept.

He promised himself from that day forward he was going to always try to be true to himself.

"If I am true to myself I will inevitably be true to others as well," thought Pouchon as he finally drifted to sleep to the soothing sounds of Mother Nature.

Many days passed without much discussion between Pouchon and Travayè. The Wiseman was busy with village concerns and did not create much time for his apprentice.

Pouchon never missed an opportunity to shadow and work alongside Travayè. He knew that his training would help him when he became king.

A few weeks later, on a resting day, Pouchon went walking along the beach with Travayè. Then as if he'd never stopped telling the story at all, Travayè talked about Truth and Freedom in the most affectionate tone.

Truth and Freedom lived a very happy life together. They reinforced and complemented each other in such a way that they essentially became one. For others, a few minutes in their presence felt like a liberating experience. That is not to say they didn't have their difficulties. Every relationship does. They just had a way of working things out for the best.

After years of blissfulness they made 'Discovery' a beautiful baby girl. She grew up to be adventurous. She married a young man, 'Exploration' and together they got 'Motivated'. Motivated married 'Excited' and that led to 'Action'. He was affectionately known as 'Right Action' because of his ancestry. Right Action met 'Intention'. He paid her a lot of attention and they got 'Desired Result' who also became known as 'Success'.

After he ended the story, Travayè didn't say much. They spent the afternoon walking the beach quietly. They enjoyed fresh coconuts while watching the sunset.

Pouchon's Journal

When I make up my mind to do something, I explore and discover the many ways I can make it happen. When those pathways are open to me, I believe more in my abilities. I have faith. I realize, "Hey, I can actually do this!"

The belief that "I can" motivates and excites me. I take action. Often, there is more than one action that I can take to achieve the same result. It is critical to take the right action.

Right action is the shortest distance between two points A and B.

Right action is integrity. It is the most efficient, most desirable way of producing a desired result. I don't have to search for the right action. It is usually right in front of me. I see it, hear it, or feel it.

To ensure the action I take is the right action I must be in balance. I must be aware. When I am aware, everything is clear.

I must listen to my inner voice. I must choose the picture that seems right to me. My inner senses will never lead me astray when I am in balance.

How can I remember to act with integrity and take right actions? I will follow this process.

Establish the desired result. Ask, what am I trying to do? What is my intention? Explore my options. There is usually more than one. As excitement builds, I choose the action that appears, feels or sounds right to me. It is normally the shortest correct distance from point A to point B.

This decision is best made when I am in Infinite-Power. It is a spirit-based decision. There is rarely a time when one single action will produce my desired result. Rather, it is a series of actions that when combined, generate the desired result.

It is important to devise a stepwise strategy that includes multiple milestones (mini desired results) and multiple actions. The process itself becomes pleasant and enjoyable. The strategy is A.I.R.: paying Attention to my Intention to achieve my desired Result.

Here is what I must do:

+ Write down my desired result.
+ Establish my time frame.
+ Determine my necessary action steps.
+ Move. Take action.
+ Enjoy! Repeat the process.

23

When the Destination is Clear, the Path Appears

— W. E. André

M any days passed. Pouchon worked and learned alongside Travayè. They had a great time working and playing together.

The beach and the waterfall were the prince's favorite places to meditate. A young villager walked toward the prince and waited until he came out of his trance.

"If everyone has the same potential, why do people who set goals not achieve them?"

"A Wise One once told me, 'when the destination is clear, the path appears,' " said the prince.

"Yes, but I know what I want to do. I even know how to do it. Still, I have no motivation to take action."

"Maybe, you ought to revisit your goals."

"Why revisit my goals if I already know what they are?"

"To make them so clear that they move you to act. When your destination is clear, your path will always be clear," said the prince.

"But they are clear," protested the young villager.

"What is it you want to do?"

"I want to be successful," said the villager.

"What does it mean to you to be successful?"

"Success, to me, is to have a lot of material possessions."

Pouchon reached into his back pocket and handed a little book to the young villager, *Ancient Wisdom for Creating Wealth*.

"Go and be successful," he said.

One late afternoon Pouchon was feeling especially insightful. He told Travayè the story of a young prince's journey.

There once was a young prince who was lost and confused about the meaning of and attainment of success. He went to his village counselor and sought his advice. The counselor told him to go and be successful. When the young prince did not attain success, he went back to the counselor who sent him on an adventure to find out how to become successful.

The young prince traveled far and wide and during his travels he learned about success and how to achieve it. The most striking revelation was that success was not at all a destination but rather a journey.

After this discovery he decided to map out the road to success and share it with others. He came up with a system for success and called it AURA.

- Awareness
- Understanding
- Responsibility
- Action

Awareness is self-realization.
Understanding is self-discovery.
Responsibility is self-accountability.
Action is self-motivation.

The young prince also recognized the difficulty of self-motivation. He designed a system to help him and others learn how to self-motivate. To make every day successful, A.I.R. is necessary. Paying Attention to Intentions produces Results. Attention is action. Intention is goal. Results is success.

Attention + Intentions = Results.

The young prince helped many islanders live life to the fullest. He became known all over the island for living every day successfully.

Travayè looked deep into Pouchon's eyes. He knew, at that moment, the prince had matured and had become a Whealthy King.

Pouchon's Journal

To my dear beloved,

Meaningless, meaningless, everything is meaningless. The only thing that matters is to remain constant in Infinite-Power.

I trust you have received the journals I sent you during my journey. I know you applied the lessons and shared them with our children, for you are a virtuous woman. I am on my way to the tiny village that does not have a Wiseman. I wish for you to join me there.

Together we can live a splendorous life and maybe others will follow our path.

The lessons came together for me during the last few moons. I have finally realized the true power of my Personal Power Grid. The only purpose of the grid is to serve as a vehicle to reach and maintain Infinite-Power. Once in Infinite-Power, I must remain true. Being true is being one with the source; I create Constant-Power.

Being in Constant-Power, I always act from Infinite-Power. I never leave the source. I finally got it. If I go out of balance I only have to apply the Rule of Thirty and use my Personal Power Grid to become one with the source and create Constant-Power.

After reaching Constant-Power I know that everything else is meaningless. I am aware of the potential of my fellow man; I understand his struggles; I respond to his needs and I take action to show him the path to constancy.

In Constant-Power I give without expecting anything back; I don't need anything. I forgive those who act against me; they are more than their behaviors. I respect others; they are as I am. I have no fear; I am with the source. I give up the need to be right; I am content. I don't compete; there is enough to fulfill my desires. I don't react to anything; the moment is perfect.

Meaningless, meaningless, everything is meaningless. The only thing that matters is constancy in Infinite-Power. I must create Constant-Power. Meaningless . . .

Today is an outstanding day!
I am aware
I am understanding
I am responsible
I am motivated
I am faithful
I am true
I am free
For in the end, it is all about me!

Part II

Creating Everyday Success

*When your desires are strong enough
you will appear to possess superhuman
powers to achieve.*

– Napoleon Hill

24

The Four Pillars of Whealth

Building Whealth

Whealth is the enjoyment of an abundance of valuable possessions, and of optimum physical and spiritual performance. Whealth is the ultimate journey.

It is a worthwhile journey. The pursuit of Whealth consists of four pillars: spiritual, financial, physical and love. When all four pillars are functioning optimally a person is primed to enjoy an abundant lifestyle. It is difficult to attain Whealth when any component is missing. They are intricately interwoven and interdependent.

Think about the human body. It is composed of many systems and organs; three of which are the heart, the liver and the brain. The body cannot exist without any one of those organs.

When one system malfunctions or goes out of balance, others are affected. The effect may not be immediate but eventually symptoms arise. Slowly the body fails and if the imbalance persists uncorrected, death ensues.

Whealth represents the body. Spirituality, finances, physical wellness and love are its systems. In order for Whealth to exist, all four pillars must function in harmony with each other and with the environment.

25

Awareness: Be Here, Now!

Recently I saw a patient—Ms. Bernie—who wanted to lose weight. In her early forties, she was having serious problems controlling her weight.

Ms. Bernie was very excited to finally get in to see me because she wanted to work with a provider who treated her whole person. As often is the case, she had lost weight many times, only to regain all the weight back, plus a few more pounds each time.

One herbal program was especially successful for her. It consisted of taking herbal supplements together with vitamins and meal replacements.

As part of this program she sold the supplements to her family and friends. Losing weight ensured her success in the business.

Focused and determined, Ms. Bernie did very well. She lost more than a hundred pounds and her business was thriving.

A few months later she became anxious, accompanied by a severe bout of depression. She decided the herbs were causing her symptoms and stopped taking them. Gradually she gained all the weight back and has been in and out of depression since.

She had a love affair with chocolate. Whenever she tried to give it up she became depressed, leading her to eat and shop excessively.

My patient was deeply religious and went to church two or three times a week. I suggested a spiritual book to her.

"I can't read it. My friends would think that it's too 'new age'," she said.

She rejected most of my suggestions, and her health did not improve. Yet she was very happy to see me every week. It gave her a sense that she was doing something about her health.

This scenario is all too common. It describes a large number of individuals. People who try everything in the book to get results yet cannot get anywhere. Nothing works for them and I suspect nothing ever will. It is not that the remedies don't work but rather the people don't believe their condition can be helped.

Often such people try one "magic method" after another in their search for the ultimate fix. They become excited about the possibility of finally achieving success. After a couple of days, sometimes maybe weeks, all interest vanishes and away they go on the quest for the next novel miracle.

In this book, when I talk about spirituality, it is not necessarily in the context of religion. Spirituality here is the pursuit of communion with the Divine. The Divine is the collective consciousness.

For some it is God. For others it is Jehovah, Allah, or Buddha. Undeniably He is the source of much joy and happiness. To know Him is truly to be free. To know Him is to know love. To know Him is to know yourself for He is within you and He is "with you always."

Though I may not be religious, I can be spiritual. To deny my spirituality is to deny myself. Spirituality is not limited to religion.

Being in communion with the Divine, I am in Infinite-Power. I am constantly communicating with the source. Once I acknowledge my source, the way to the Divine will reveal itself to me.

Science theorizes that my body is made of information stored in the form of DNA. This DNA is passed down to me from my parents who got it from their parents, who got it from their parents and so on. Though I may not be an exact replica of my father, I have a lot of his DNA in me.

My grandparents' DNA, my great grandparents' DNA and all my ancestors' combine to make me who I am today.

My brother and my two sisters have part of my father and of my ancestors. So even though we are separate people, we are the same.

This idea—all people share a common consciousness—I learned twenty-five years ago in Sunday school. Yet only recently did I understand the true meaning of it.

I wanted peace, but I got conflict. I desired riches but I had misfortunes. I searched high and low to no avail. God was not granting my wishes.

Then it occurred to me. *If God is my father and he owns the universe then that must mean everything I need I already have. All my desires are within my reach. Better yet, all my desires have already been fulfilled. Since He is within me I also own everything He does.*

How dare I compare myself to the Divine? I am but a lowly creature that does not deserve to be even mentioned. When I realized this was not the case, I understood the power available to me.

Excited about my new awareness, I shared it with a very good friend I have known for over twenty years. He looked at me in disbelief, shaking his head.

"You should really be careful what you say," he said with grave concern. "That sounds a lot like blasphemy."

"I understand your point. For years I thought the same way," I said.

"And you should continue to think that way."

"Even though it is written in the Bible over and over ..."

"Man," he interrupted, "I can't even fathom the idea that God is in me."

"I know what you mean," I pushed. "I felt that any mention of God and me should be done with me in a subordinate position, not as an integral part of Him. Until I read this in the scripture.

> *Then God said, "Let us make man in our image, in our likeness, and let them rule over the fish of the sea and the birds of the air, over the livestock, over all the earth and over all the creatures that move along the ground."*
> — Genesis 1:26

Jesus went further when he said, "And surely I will be with you always…"

— Matthew 28:20

My friend did not take kindly to this explanation. I understood his predicament. Accepting that the Divine is within me can be too heavy a burden to carry. It means I have to stop doubting. I can no longer discriminate. I have to start believing in my abilities. I have to accept others as my equal. It means my neighbor's failure is my failure.

I have to watch my diet, exercise and take care of my mind and body. It means *the buck stops here*.

When I belittle myself, I demean the Divine. Anything I do to myself, I do to the Divine. How can I harm myself without hurting Him? My actions not only affect me but they influence the universe in general.

The first step in the pursuit of spirituality is the practice of awareness and acceptance. I must be aware of my potential and learn to accept it as fact. I must practice self-awareness and self-acceptance. Being aware, I am closer to communion with the Divine. No more conflict, just peace.

I see things for what they are; not what I want them to be nor what I wish they were. I realize each moment in time is perfect. I learned of this concept from *The Way of the Buddha*. Deepak Chopra, MD, does an excellent job of explaining it in his book, the *Seven Spiritual Laws of Success*.

Every moment is as it should be. The past, present and future are all here in this moment, right here, right now. The decisions I made yesterday determined what I am doing today. What I do today determines what I will be doing tomorrow. Everything that I have done my entire life led me to this moment.

What I am doing this very moment determines my future. To struggle against the moment is to struggle against all the forces of nature that have conspired to bring about the moment. What a powerful concept. Go back, read it again.

This concept applies to everything I do in life. I remember a young woman that I once worked with in a small but busy clinic. She was an excellent worker. She could hold down that clinic all by herself while we saw up to fifty patients in one day.

Sometimes she went out in the middle of the week, dancing and drinking until the wee hours of the morning. I could always tell when she had had a good time the previous night.

She showed up at work tired and moody. She didn't perform her normal duties. Each time she got severely sick and then missed a day of work. At the end of the week her paycheck reflected the missed day. She then complained how she never had enough money.

There are decisions that are affecting me in the present that I did not make. They may have been made by my bosses, teachers, spouse, government or centuries ago by my ancestors.

Rather than worry about what I can't change, I focus on this fact. *I now have the power to make better choices.*

26

The Extra Step

The next step is the practice of understanding. This involves taking the extra step. Let me explain. A few years ago I decided to form a mastermind group, a weekly meeting with like-minded people to discuss self-improvement. I explained the concept to a couple of my friends and asked if they wanted to participate.

After a brief discussion we decided it was a worthwhile idea. We agreed on a date for our first meeting and everyone was to read *The Power of Focus* by Jack Canfield and company.

By our third session we were having serious difficulty communicating. "Feelings" were getting in the way.

Then one Saturday morning as we sat there talking, almost at an impasse, someone said it.

"I don't understand."

It was as if the whole thing blew open. Until that day we were operating based on our own previous experiences. We spent the majority of our time interpreting each other's words based on our past experiences and our own point of view.

Since that morning we got into the habit of asking for explanation and pacing each other to make sure we understood exactly what we were saying to each other.

"In all things seek knowledge, but more so seek understanding."

Practicing understanding helps me on my path to building Whealth. It helps me to act instead of react. Recall the earlier discussion on self-awareness and self-acceptance. When I am aware of my potential, when I accept myself as I am, I know I am just as I should be, *perfect*.

Everything I need is within me. I need "understanding" to help me realize that since I am perfect, there is nothing anyone can give to me I don't already possess.

No one can take anything away from me. It is all mine; my birth-given gift and it will be with me always. Why would anyone want to take something from me he already possesses? Everyone is the same and has the same potential. Everyone is perfect.

Everything I need, I have. It cannot be taken away from me. Understanding this helps me release the fear of loss, the fear of being inadequate or not measuring up. I learn to set my own standards and I am confident I can meet them because the power is within me. As I build confidence I open myself up for more challenges and opportunities.

This happened to me a short while ago. While practicing medicine I noticed I was not enjoying my profession. I wanted to help people heal, physically, mentally and spiritually. But this did not seem the way to do it. I felt I was in the wrong field.

My mood, during my workday, depended on the type of patients I treated. I thoroughly enjoyed patients who came to me for weight loss or wellness medicine. I talked to them at length and counseled them on proper nutrition, mental and physical fitness.

What was happening to me? I had wanted to practice medicine since I was a child. Why wasn't I enjoying my job?

The answer came to me simply. My true desire is to help people heal. This involves the whole person: body, mind and spirit. Because the practice of medicine is so focused on the physical, it does not allow me to address all three dimensions of healing. This was the source of my frustration and disenchantment. I did not feel that I was doing much good for my patients.

As I moved from awareness to understanding of my predicament I opened myself to suggestions from the Divine. The answers were always with me. I was being groomed for this moment ever since I was a child and probably even before then.

I saw the patterns of my life in the choices I made. It seemed one way or another I always gravitated toward the path of being a promoter of healing. Even my supposed failures led me in that direction. As my path became clearer, so did my options. I no longer felt like I was locked in. The doors opened. I had options.

Practicing understanding is simple. It involves taking an extra step before acting on anything. Most of my previous responses to situations were reactions; I did not take the extra step. The extra step consists simply of pausing for a brief moment and asking, "Do I understand?"

This is not hesitation. There is no fear or doubt associated with the pause. It is totally deliberate and purposeful. When I do this, I ensure I do not speak out of turn. I don't react to situations, or make hasty and harmful decisions. I expand my options by seeing every event from each position on my Personal Power Grid.

It greatly improves my communication with the Divine, and with the people who are close to me. Do this regularly and your performance will soar.

27

The Buck Stops Here

The next step toward Whealth is the practice of responsibility. I know in all matters I have the responsibility to act. With the ability to respond or responsibility, come choices. With choices come consequences. This is normally known as "cause and effect." In this system cause and effect are outmoded. Here, I stop, I think and I act with congruence.

A friend of mine, Al, a thirty-seven-year-old Hispanic man has been working for a major chain retail store for the past two years.

He is married and has two kids. Al is going through a major financial crisis, intensified by what he calls the constant "nagging" of his wife about money. He feels trapped and cannot see a way out.

Al has numerous problems with the upper management team at work. It seems to Al every time something is missing in the store, fingers automatically point at him. Although he likes his job he is finding it increasingly difficult to enjoy his daily duties as a member of the management team.

Al is experiencing anxiety, mood swings and depression.

This case presents an interesting dilemma. I know Al from previous encounters and he is a very intelligent person.

"I feel like I'm surrounded by idiots. I hate having to constantly explain myself to people," he said.

Al is very critical of himself but more so of others. He does not have many friends at work. Al thinks the world is out to get him and the only reason he is not already rich is because of oppression from the system.

I carefully listen to Al explain his situation.

"What do you think you should do?" I ask him.

In a burst of anger he answers, "Quit my job and leave the wife!"

"I have another plan you can try. How about going to work for one week and pretending you are someone else."

"What the hell is that going to prove? I'm not going to do that."

"Al, you have the 'response-ability' to deal with the situation. You have many choices including not making any. When situations arise you choose how you want to deal with them. The easiest solution is to blame your problems on circumstances you think are out of your control or on everyone else."

"I never make excuses, man," Al protests. "My alarm clock fails, my car breaks down, traffic is bad a lot of times, my boss hates me, my wife is just a nagger and I simply don't make enough money."

"You see my point now Al? By 'passing the buck' you feel you don't have to deal with the situation. Nothing could be further from the truth."

Al is not the only person to do this. This type of approach leads to inaction and inaction leads to further detriment. This is a suicidal mindset.

Many patients come to my office with illnesses that must have started months, sometime years before. But they never sought care because they thought their illnesses would "go away" if they ignored them.

Al is on a similar path. His depression and anxiety are closely related to his difficulties at work and at home. Soon he complained of upset stomach and chronic pain.

"It's funny," he tells me, "my pain is worse when I get ready to go to work and it is much better as soon as I leave work."

The first step in exercising responsibility is to look at myself. I take a long hard look in the mirror. That person staring back at me has a lot to do with what's going on with me. He is the only one responsible for all that is happening to me. The "buck" really does stop here.

I'm reminded of Cathy, a young lady I once worked with, who continuously ranted and raved that her best friend was about to marry a man she only met six months ago. The fellow had no place of his own to live and he was cheating and disrespecting her friend.

As I sat there listening to her I was amazed how upset she was about her friend's predicament. Cathy was in a bad relationship as well. Her fiancé was cheating and disrespecting her.

"What bothers me most about other people is often what I don't like about myself and feel powerless to change," I thought to myself.

I have a choice how I respond to any given situation. Anytime I have to make a decision, I first look inward. No one has the power to dictate my actions. Where and who I am today is a culmination of all my previous choices. Situations cannot dictate my response. However, my past experiences can lead me to reactions.

The scenario presents itself and I decide whether to be angry, upset, happy, or joyful. By focusing on myself, I am less likely to blame others for my misfortunes. I am more likely to accept responsibility to take appropriate actions.

I tried to explain this to Al.

"How is it my fault these people act the way they do?" he asked.

"It isn't," I told him. "But how you respond is up to you. Pretend to be someone else for a week at work. What I mean is I want you to pretend to be someone people on your job like. Whenever something is said or done that you think is unfair, try looking at it through the eyes of this new 'likeable' guy and see if there is any other explanation for what you see as unfairness."

I wanted Al to look inside and see what type of issues he had with himself.

We often create problems or situations based on our own beliefs and past experiences. That is a source of a lot of misunderstandings and miscommunications. It is difficult not to get upset when someone does something we perceive as being disrespectful. Since we were previously in a similar situation, our instinct is to feel slighted. Similar actions may not be taken with similar intents. When we look inward we place ourselves in a position to realize the obvious; it is all about us.

Two weeks after our conversation, Al came back to see me.

"This thing you asked me to do messed with my mind," he said with a smile. "It was difficult at first to practice being someone else. I had to constantly remind myself I was this new person. Once I got it down, my whole outlook changed."

The old cushion was gone. Al had to find other explanation for his feelings.

"Man, I realized that I wasn't nice to my co-workers. But you know, I started saying good morning and smiling more at my customers. Would you believe it, they started being all kinds of nice to me."

"Why do you think that is, Al?"

"I think I was afraid, man. I didn't want people getting in my business or getting too close to me. It was safer when I hid behind my feelings. That way I didn't have to take responsibility. Once I became someone else I had no choice but to face my fears."

"So did that fix all your problems at work?"

"I must tell you that I still think some of the people at work get treated differently based on their skin color. But by taking responsibility for myself, I'm able to make better choices and more productive decisions."

This did not just work for Al. It has worked for me in different circumstances and it can work for anyone. Nothing is lost by trying.

28

Knowledge Without Action = Death

Once I am aware, I understand the dynamics involved and accept responsibility that it is time to take action. When I follow the previous three steps correctly, the right action always reveals itself. I still hold the power to take the right or wrong action but at least I know the choice is mine. Taking the right action ensures I am in constant communication with the Divine.

A few years ago I was teaching a Sunday Bible class. One day we were discussing how to honor God in everything we do. It was a difficult task to figure out exactly what that meant. Most members in the class including myself could not get the concept. How do I honor God every moment of every day?

One class member stated life would be boring if she had to go around all day acting like she was a saint. That's when it hit me. Being in communion with the Divine is not boring and does not entail "going around acting like a saint" all day. All it involves is to try to take the right action in the moment; whether it is at work, at home, having a meal or reading a book.

How can I practice right action consistently? Once I realize what the right action is, it is helpful to remember to get some "A.I.R." (Attention + Intention = Results). I must breathe easily and consistently. There is something very eloquent about breathing. It is the only act I perform that can be totally voluntary or involuntary.

My body can function for days, even weeks without water. Jesus fasted forty nights and forty days. There are reports of people surviving even longer periods without food or water.

Yet the brain begins to wither and die after just a few minutes without oxygen. Breathing helps the mind to relax. It calms down the senses. It helps me think clearly. It even acts as a pain killer.

There are proper breathing techniques to help relieve anxiety, stress, asthma, and birth labor pain. Improper breathing—when the lungs do not fully expand—can be detrimental to good health. Too much oxygen can be fatal, just as too little.

The useful form of oxygen is obtained through oxidation. This process also produces a harmful byproduct—free radicals—responsible for aging, cancer and heart disease, to name a few. Oxygen is the reason why people take antioxidants to prevent illnesses and premature aging.

Improper breathing can lead to chronic pain, as in the mother who never recovers from giving birth, or the person who develops cancer.

The key points to remember about breathing are that it is essential to sustain life and it can be voluntary or involuntary.

If I pay attention to my breathing for just a few minutes each day I can greatly improve my health. If I do not take care of my breathing, it will go on anyway but it may not be optimal.

To stay alive I must breathe properly and consistently.

Imagine the quality of life I would achieve if I breathed properly and consistently. I might reach the biblical lifeline; I might live to be one hundred and fifty years old.

The same is true of giving attention to intention. The more consistent I am the better my results will be. Most of us have jobs that we go to on a daily basis. Our paychecks reflect our consistency on the job. By showing up every day (and maybe doing some work) we get a consistent paycheck. Much more can be said about consistency. The main idea is to *be regularly regular paying attention to my intention.*

To be successful at practicing right action, I must pay attention to the A.I.R. I breathe.

The acronym A.I.R. stands for Attention, Intention, and Result. Paying attention to my intention leads to good results. Once I know the right action, it becomes my intention. It is what I intend to do. Intention brings result when it gets attention. All the best intentions will not get proper results unless I pay attention to them.

Attention therefore is the "doing" part. It is the movement, the "get up and go." It is what converts intention into result.

Suppose my intention is to have money. Attention may be to get a job, open a business, or get a degree. If my intention is to lose weight, my attention is to eat right and exercise.

To stay thin I must be consistent with my diet and exercise. It's just like breathing. I do it constantly and consistently. I may not do it properly all the time, but I do it nevertheless.

Remember there is no such thing as inaction. Choosing not to, is an action in itself. Inaction produces results that may be detrimental. Consistent inaction leads to death: physical, mental and spiritual.

This is evident in my daily life. When I choose to be irresponsible and complacent I cause pain to myself, those around me and the Divine. Irregular, improper attention to my intention also leads to death.

Once I know the right action and manifest my intention, I discover the proper attention to be given to my intention. This is a most beautiful aspect of nature. All I have to do is let my intention be known and the how and the when are revealed.

Therefore do not worry about tomorrow, for tomorrow will worry about itself. Each day has enough trouble of its own.

– Matthew 6:34

Have you ever decided you wanted to make a change in your life? You had no idea where or how to proceed but you knew that was the right action. Miraculously, you met people, got information, and learned ways to perform your task in the most unusual places.

When I finally accepted my God-given gift of caring for others, I was graced with a similar blessing. Step-by-step and effortlessly I was guided through the entire path. Whenever I deviated, whenever I took my mind off my goal, I immediately knew it. I struggled. All the signs guided me back to my previous step.

After manifesting my intention, several doors opened for me. I was working in a medical clinic where the primary focus was on business. Patient care was not important. As a matter of fact patients were deliberately given substandard care so they returned for follow up.

In just a few weeks I felt anxious when it was time to go to work. I had back pain, upset stomach and sometimes dizziness. I knew deep within me I did not like my job and I felt guilty and sorry for the many patients who came there.

My financial situation was on life support. I needed my job. To leave that job would be financial suicide. The only thing worse than working at that clinic, was losing my job.

Finally, I decided I had to do "something." Jobs were not found easily in my field. It could take a while before I was employed again. I decided to follow my true calling and become a wellness guru.

Concerned about bills and very much in debt, I left my full-time job and worked part-time. I began to search for other work as a Physician Assistant two days after quitting my former job. I was amazed how the doors of opportunity flew open. I had many options but I needed to know there would be a paycheck on Friday.

Then one night in the midst of my confusion, I had a very revealing dream. I was wandering around in the city where I lived. I drove to many strange places then went home. The next day I drove around again. This time I was lost and trying to find my way home. But because of the aimless driving I did the day before, I was able to find my way home without much effort or frustration.

The meaning of this dream was not immediately apparent to me. But as I thought about it, I realized all the answers I was looking for were already there. All I had to do was look around. I had been there before and I knew what to do; embrace the uncertainty and release the fear.

I was worried about not being able to pay the bills or ending up with no telephone or electricity. I was terrified of what my wife would think of me for putting my family in that same situation again. I felt resentment at the world because I did not have enough money to simply quit my job and start my own business.

Once I became aware of these feelings, I was able to face the situation. This fear was not new. It was not unfounded. It was a learned behavior. It came from previous experiences. *Anything I am afraid of, I will have to face sooner or later. Not only will I face it, I will also overcome it.*

Fears are based on past experiences. No one wants to make the same mistake twice. As a safety mechanism, the subconscious goes into red alert each time I face a situation that has caused me pain or discomfort before.

This makes me hesitant; I become anxious and take wrong action. Sometimes the fear is based on previous experiences my friends, families or parents have experienced. I witnessed their pain and suffering and I do not wish to experience the same.

This reminds me of stories from my native country, Haiti, about the making of slaves. Pregnant slave women were taken to a field with their spouses. The husbands were tortured to death while their pregnant wives watched.

This atrocity was to instill fear in the mothers and essentially pass it on to their babies; an unborn child grew up fearing the slave masters, never knowing why.

I think it's called "unfounded" fear; "unfounded" because the slave breeders didn't directly physically harm these children.

It's possible to be fearful of situations I haven't personally encountered. I may not readily know the origins of my fears but I know they are not "unfounded."

Since I have previous experiences with the fears I face, I already know how to deal with them; successfully at that. I should avoid running away from my fears. Only by facing them will I ever find ways to successfully cope with them.

I realized, even though I was decreasing my household income, I still had plenty and with faith I would eventually have more. I applied the A.U.R.A. system, followed my inner voice and moved on.

Be sure you are in balance all the time.

There is a way that seems right to a man,
but in the end it leads to death.

– Proverbs 14:12

29

I Did It My Way

Beep, beep, beep. 5:30 in the morning. I don't feel
like getting up. I don't like what this day has in
store for me. It's raining outside. Raindrops on the
window blur my vision. I can't see clearly. I haven't been seeing clearly
since the last time I saw my editor. Oh yeah, that witch! Always on my
back, pushing, pulling, tugging …

Drip, drip, drip. Raindrops fall on the window seal.

Beep, beep, beep! The alarm clock screams. I don't want to get up.
It's not safe outside my bed. The silk sheets caress my stiffening body.
Safety, familiarity, this is comfort.

Beep, beep, beep. My wife shifts in the bed. The buzzing sound
disturbs her early morning dreams. But I don't want to get up; it's not
comfortable out there, I have to think and do work.

I have been writing this book, on and off, for almost five years now.
It has consumed my life. The past eleven months have been "H, E,
double hockey sticks." It's time to move on.

Six months to my 35th birthday and my goals are slipping away.
This book consumes my life.

Jab! I feel the stabbing pain on my left side, between the second and
the third rib.

"Okay, okay!"

I reluctantly roll out of bed and amble to the bathroom to turn off the
alarm clock. Tear drops, from the rain, drip down the windows. Leaning

over the sink, staring in the mirror, disheveled, discouraged, I can't do this anymore ... wait ... I must be dreaming.

"Hey papa!" I open my eyes. My two year old son stands next to the bed. "Where mommy?"

Yes, I was dreaming. This all took place in my mind's eye.

"Good morning, sexy piece of heaven." She comes walking out of the bathroom smiling broadly at me.

"I've got to get up," I say half awake, "I have a nine o'clock meeting with my editor."

Stay focused, work your plan. Do what you can. The rest will fall into place. Growth is never safe. It requires faith, constancy and dedication. Be willing to be okay with uncertainty. Get comfortable being out of your comfort zone. Know that everything will be okay. When you feel like giving up, stand your ground. When you think you have done enough, push a little harder.

The loftier your goal becomes, the heavier your burden may be. Sometimes, it may feel like it's you against the world, you have no ally. The price may appear too much to pay. But you must keep on keeping on, go the distance. You must be outstanding.

There is a certain sense of accomplishment that comes from knowing you did your best. You can stand in front of the mirror and know that everything is as it should be; you kept your end of the bargain.

Emptiness and resentment surface when you doubt your performance. The small voice inside echoes all the things you chose not to do. It is like having a checklist on your mind with unchecked items. It fogs your brain. You develop self-doubt and hesitation. Your self-worth diminishes. Your self-confidence is shot. Soon you start thinking you are not good enough. Maybe you bit off more than you could chew. After about the ninth time you think it, you start speaking it. It becomes a belief. *I'm not good enough. I'm not deserving. I will never reach my goals.*

Growth requires the acuity to identify what is working and what is not. Basic keys to success include knowing your purpose, working your purpose, and the acumen to recognize unwanted outcomes and adjust your plans.

When times are tough, as they often are, take an inventory of your successes. What have you accomplished so far? Relive the experiences that bolster your self esteem. Reevaluate your current position. Is there an unwanted outcome? How did it happen? What must be done to adjust your course? Step back, evaluate, and then proceed with clear purposeful goals.

30

Seven "Truths" That Keep You Poor

1. Life is hard.

Each person is given a gift at birth which when used properly, will propel them to unimaginable heights. Everyone has the same potential to be successful. When you find and fulfill your purpose, your needs are effortlessly met.

2. It's okay to fail.

Many books proclaim failure is a necessary step to success; there can be no success without failure. This is not true. You fail only when you give up. There are no failures; only unwanted results. If something is not producing the intended result, do something else. Keep trying until the goal is attained.

3. Life is a struggle.

There are no struggles in life. When goals are clear, actions are smooth. If you are struggling you need to reevaluate your goals. You struggle when you take your mind off your dreams and concentrate on the distracters. A bump on the journey of success, and down you go; you give up trying. Keep your mind on the journey.

4. Persist and succeed.

Persistence is not enough. Identify what works and what doesn't work. Abandon the actions that produce unwanted results and embrace those that yield desired results.

5. Serve others and succeed.

A sick doctor cannot care for his patients. A tired pilot cannot safely fly a plane. Serve others through self-service. Take the time to find purpose. When you find it, serve others by fulfilling that purpose.

6. We can't all be captains.

Why not? There are plenty of boats and a vast ocean out there. You are responsible for your boat. To float or sink depends entirely on you.

7. Not everyone is born to be successful.

Success is not a prize reserved for an elite few. It is a birthright. Everyone can be successful. The only question is, are you going to assert your birthright?

31

Living with Purpose

Success is personal. It means different things to different people. Many books proclaim to know the formula for success. If the meaning of success is different for each person, can any one book or program give away the secret to a successful life? Can any one person show another how to achieve something so personal?

No one can show you how to be successful; no one has ever achieved the level of success you are attempting to reach. Since success is uniquely yours, no one can give it to you.

What is similar among all people is an innate desire to succeed. Some act on it, others don't. But the desire remains. You experience the world in the same way everyone else does, through your senses. You see, feel, hear, taste and smell your way through life. If you lack one sense, your body compensates.

This basic similarity links everyone together. It enables you to model other people's behavior, and follow in their footsteps to accomplish anything.

John is a twenty-nine-year-old entrepreneur who wants to become a millionaire importing and exporting goods. Though he studied business and marketing in college he has no real life knowledge on how to proceed. Through a mentoring program, John meets Pierre, a multi-millionaire who makes his money in real estate.

Even though Pierre's experience is in real estate he is able to mentor John and teach him the principles of success. He does this by laying down the foundation of a successful mind.

Whether you want to become fit, get a college degree or build a multi-million dollar empire, the basics remain the same. It starts with planning and setting self-fulfilling goals. The energy it takes to plan and set clear goals will save you time and money.

Imagine going on a trip with a vague idea of your destination and no map showing you how to get there. This is exactly what happens when you undertake any project without first setting goals.

There is more to goal-setting than just writing a list on a piece of paper. You will succeed faster when you set clear goals. A clear goal is a self-fulfilling one. It is self-fulfilling because *when your goal is clear, the means appear*.

Hondas were always my favorite cars. My first car was a Honda Civic hatchback that I bought in high school. I have since owned five Hondas in the last fifteen years. After graduating college my wife and I needed a second vehicle. We wanted a truck so we decided on a Jeep. From that day on I only noticed Jeeps on the road.

You may have had a similar experience where one event opens your eyes to something else. This awakening opens your mind to the possibilities. This is awareness. It's exactly what happens when goals are clear. Suddenly, the many ways to achieve your desire appear; people with resources cross your path. It is as if the entire universe has come together to help you achieve your goal.

The only way to set clear goals is with purpose. True success comes from living with purpose. Through modeling other people's successful behavior you can achieve anything; money, riches and good health. You gain meaning only from living purposefully.

What is purpose? Jesus was born with the purpose of saving mankind; it determined the lifestyle He led. It required Him to be humble, modest, caring and dedicated. Jesus handled difficulties faithfully. He had purpose; the goals were clear, the means appeared and He turned obstacles into opportunities.

Martin Luther King and Joan of Arc also had purpose, the fire within. Toussaint L'Ouverture, the leader of the slave revolution in Haiti, said when he was captured by the French, "Killing me is like cutting the trunk of a tree. Its roots are deep and many and the tree will rise again."

Purpose is not something you choose. It chooses you. It is what you were born to do. It is a cause. When you act with purpose you act with integrity. You show universal love. Though you may suffer both physically and mentally, you will never fail. Success is inevitable.

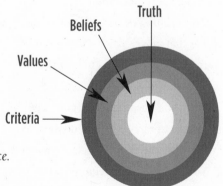

Criteria are the reasons we do the things we do.
I work to make money.

Values are the things that are important to us.
I value financial independence.

Beliefs are the things we accept as truth without positive knowledge.
Financial independence creates freedom.

Truth is purpose. It gives meaning to life. It is a mandate.
I want to help others realize their potential.

All criteria lead to purpose. I work to make money because I value family togetherness. I believe taking care of my family promotes togetherness. I fulfill my purpose by caring for my family and promoting togetherness. People who witness my success and realize they have the same potential can model my behavior and become successful.

You are here to fulfill a need. This need relates to your foundation. Everyone shares the same source. You and I are one.

When you are born into this world you become an individual, you are separate. Your ultimate mission is to preserve the oneness.

How to serve is your responsibility. You don't choose it, you must find it. It's always there. After all you are a "commissioned" officer in the army of oneness. You just have to accept your orders and carry them out.

Everyone is given different means to achieve their goal; some become doctors and carpenters while others farm or teach. Each one is "the one." This is understanding.

Open your eyes, listen attentively, pay attention to your inner feelings. What moves you? What's been following you around since you were a child and refuses to let go? If you could change anything in this world, what would it be?

Once you know your purpose, you can then determine the action you must take to carry out your mission. What state do you need to be in? What resources do you need? Where will you find them?

Your purpose may require you to become a millionaire. It may necessitate a billionaire to give away all material possessions.

Are you willing to accept your mission? Will you take the call to action?

32

Finding Meaning

This is where you list your goals and dreams. Follow each step exactly.

1. Go back to the earliest time you can remember having dreams (infancy to age ten). Write them down. Make a list of the top five dreams you had under each category: health, wealth, relationship (love) and spirituality. Do it now! Go!

When I grow up I want to:	
Health	**Wealth** EXAMPLE
Be a model	Be rich
Play sports	Own a mansion
Be the fastest man in the world	Have an elevator in my home
Swim across the ocean	Have a yacht
Leap like a frog	Have lots of shoes
Love	**Spirituality**
Get married	Live forever
Have children	Meet God
Have a big, beautiful wedding	Save the world
Never fight	Feed the poor
Have a beautiful mate	Be a psychic

When I grow up I want to:

Health

1. _____
2. _____
3. _____
4. _____
5. _____

Wealth

1. _____
2. _____
3. _____
4. _____
5. _____

Love

1. _____
2. _____
3. _____
4. _____
5. _____

Spirituality

1. _____
2. _____
3. _____
4. _____
5. _____

2. List all the things you dream of doing now. Dream big; let
   your imagination run wild. If you had the power to do or
   achieve anything you want to achieve, what would it be?
   Dream bigger; if you knew you could not fail what would you
   want to do? List any and everything you wish to do. Just as
   before, your list should include all four pillars of life: health,
   wealth, relationship (love) and spirituality. Do it now! Go!

1. _____

2. _____

3. _____

4. _____

5. _____

6. _____

7. _____

8. _____

9. _____

10. _____

3. Your next step is to compare your two lists of dreams.
How many of your dreams are listed on both lists? Write
down any dream that is similar on a new list. Do it now! Go!

1. _____

2. _____

3. _____

4. _____

5. _____

6. _____

7. _____

8. _____

9. _____

10. _____

4. Somewhere on the list you just created, you will find your true purpose in life.

    a. Prioritize this list to create your Purpose Power List. Take a good look at it. What jumps out at you? Something in there has been following you since you were a child and has refused to go away. What is it? What will you do about it?

    b. Keep the top ten items on your list. If you have fewer than ten dreams on your Purpose Power List, add anything you want to do, any dreams you have that are not currently on the list.

PURPOSE POWER LIST

1.
2.
3.
4.
5.
6.
7.
8.
9.
10.

c.   The next step is to understand your dreams. For each item
     on your list, write down your criteria. Then de-layer it to
     its core, its deepest intent.

EXAMPLE

Dream	I want to:	be a millionaire
Criteria	Because	I want financial independence
Value	Because	I want to be free
Belief	Because	I can help others be free
Intent	So that	Everyone can be free

1.

Dream	I want to:	
Criteria	Because	
Value	Because	
Belief	Because	
Intent	So that	

2.

Dream	I want to:	
Criteria	Because	
Value	Because	
Belief	Because	
Intent	So that	

3.

Dream	I want to:	
Criteria	Because	
Value	Because	
Belief	Because	
Intent	So that	

4.

Dream	I want to:	
Criteria	Because	
Value	Because	
Belief	Because	
Intent	So that	

5.

Dream	I want to:	
Criteria	Because	
Value	Because	
Belief	Because	
Intent	So that	

d. How many of your dreams have similar deepest intent? Which one is most important to you? _____

e. If your deepest intent came from an infinite source, where would you say it came from? _____

33

The Five Levels of Power

Personal power is the ability to remain constant, regardless of the circumstances. A person who is constant in Infinite-Power, masters his destiny.

You can use the power grid to create unlimited personal power. This system, when applied correctly, can lead to great success in every aspect of life.

Each person has a Power Grid. This grid has five positions. Self-Power—experiencing the world from your own point of view; Other-Power—experiencing the world from someone else's point of view; Third-Power—experiencing the world from the point of view of a detached observer; Integral-Power—experiencing the world from an insider's point of view; and Infinite Power—being one with the source.

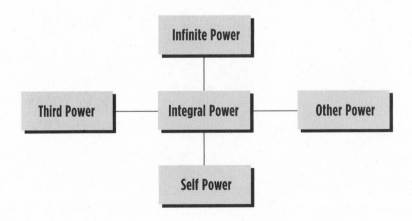

Review your Purpose Power List. Look at your intents from each position on your Personal Power Grid. Do they pass the Infinite-Power test? Do they benefit everyone?

Your Purpose Power List is a very powerful tool. You have given life to your intentions.

34

Setting Goals With Vision

People don't plan to fail,
rather they fail to plan.

Goal setting is the key to success. When goals are properly set, they act as a magnet pulling you toward your desired outcome. It is essential to set purposeful goals.

When setting goals there are certain basic questions that must be answered:

+ Where are you now? (health, wealth, love, spiritual)

+ Where do you want to be?
  State your goals in positive terms.
  Be thorough and specific.
  What do you really want?

+ What will you see, hear and feel when you achieve your goal?
  Is your goal compelling?
  Does it pull you?

Once all these questions are answered, it is time for a balance check.

+ Does your goal fit in with your belief system? (health, wealth, love, spiritual)

+ What will you gain?

+ What will you give up?

As you answer these questions, notice how your body responds in terms of images, sounds and feelings.

✦ Cartesian Logic

What will happen if I achieve my goal?

What will happen if I don't achieve my goal?

What won't happen if I achieve my goal?

What won't happen if I don't achieve my goal?

Goals 101

The first step in setting compelling goals is to realize where you are now. Then decide where you want to be. State your goals in positive terms. Be thorough and specific. What do you really want?

EXAMPLE

Where I am now	Where I want to be
Making minimum wage	Taking home $1,000 a week
Single	Married with a son and daughter
50 pounds overweight	Weigh 135 pounds in one year
Not giving back	Give $400 monthly to charity

Fill in the blanks on the next page. When you are writing about where you want to be, be sure to dream big. If you could do anything you want to do; if you could be anyone you want to be. If there were no possibility of failure, what would you try; who would you be?

GOALS

Where I am now:

_____

_____

_____

_____

_____

_____

_____

_____

_____

_____

_____

_____

_____

Where I want to be:

_____

_____

_____

_____

_____

_____

_____

_____

_____

_____

_____

_____

_____

Do a Balance Check

Does your goal fit your belief system? Belief is the mental acceptance of something as truth without positive knowledge.

Beliefs come from childhood experiences, traumas and recurring experiences. Beliefs help you make sense of the world. They help guide you through your journey.

Whether you succeed or fail depends on what you believe. A person who believes life is hard, acts as though it is true. As you believe, so you will sow; as you sow so you will reap.

What do you BELIEVE about:	
Health	**Wealth**
1.	1.
2.	2.
3.	3.
4.	4.
5.	5.
Love	**Spirituality**
1.	1.
2.	2.
3.	3.
4.	4.
5.	5.

Now compare your goals to your beliefs. Are there any conflicts?

Values define what is important to us. Just like beliefs, we acquire them from childhood. Values motivate us.

What do you VALUE about your:	
Health	**Wealth**
1.	1.
2.	2.
3.	3.
4.	4.
5.	5.
Love	**Spirituality**
1.	1.
2.	2.
3.	3.
4.	4.
5.	5.

Now compare your goals to your values. Are there any conflicts? Suppose your goal is to make plenty of money and that requires you to work long hours. Presume that you value time with your family. You now have a conflict. How do you resolve this conflict?

What will you GAIN when you achieve your goals?

Health

1. _____
2. _____
3. _____
4. _____
5. _____

Wealth

1. _____
2. _____
3. _____
4. _____
5. _____

Love

1. _____
2. _____
3. _____
4. _____
5. _____

Spirituality

1. _____
2. _____
3. _____
4. _____
5. _____

As you answer the next question, notice how your body responds in terms of images, sounds and feelings.

What will you LOSE when you achieve your goals?

Health

1. _____
2. _____
3. _____
4. _____
5. _____

Wealth

1. _____
2. _____
3. _____
4. _____
5. _____

Love

1. _____
2. _____
3. _____
4. _____
5. _____

Spirituality

1. _____
2. _____
3. _____
4. _____
5. _____

Cartesian Logic

What will happen if I achieve my goal?

_____
_____
_____

René Descartes
(1596-1650)

_____
_____

What will happen if I don't achieve my goal?

_____
_____
_____
_____
_____

What will not happen if I achieve my goal?

_____
_____
_____
_____
_____

What will not happen if I don't achieve my goal?

_____
_____
_____
_____
_____

Mind and body are part of the same system. They are interconnected and they influence each other continuously. Your physiological state and your mental state are interdependent.

People speak of the "wrong mindset" or being in the "right state of mind." A state of mind is all the sounds, images, feelings and physiology a person experiences and expresses in the moment.

You struggle when the mind-body (ego-spirit) equilibrium goes out of balance. That limits choices. Acting with ego is acting fearfully. That is a non-resourceful state.

Spirit is giving. Acting in spirit is love. That is a resourceful state. Choices are limitless.

101 Obstacles

What is keeping you from achieving your goals?

Health

_____
_____
_____
_____
_____

Wealth

_____
_____
_____
_____
_____

Love

_____
_____
_____
_____
_____

Spirituality

_____
_____
_____
_____
_____

35

Building Power Resources

+ What state of mind will you have to be in to achieve your goals? Will you have to be curious, motivated, flexible, assertive, ingenious, loving, and alert?

+ Have you ever met anyone who has achieved this goal before?

+ Have you ever achieved this goal before?

Health

_____

_____

_____

_____

Wealth

_____

_____

_____

_____

Love

_____

_____

_____

_____

Spirituality

_____

_____

_____

_____

(Make sure your resources do not depend on someone else.)

Picture Yourself Having Achieved Your Goal.

Wealth

What is your education level? _____

What do you do for a living? _____

What is your net worth? _____

How much liquid cash do you have? _____

How much money is in your emergency fund? _____

Do you save regularly? _____

Do you give to charity? _____

What is in your portfolio? _____

What city do you live in? _____

Where is your primary residence? _____

Describe your primary residence. _____

Do you have any other houses? Where? _____

Describe your other houses. _____

What kind of car do you drive? (year, make, model)

_____

How many cars do you own? _____

Do you own a boat? _____

Do you own plane? _____

Do you own a helicopter? _____

Any other type of vehicles? _____

Where do you prefer to shop for clothes? _____

for food? _____

for shoes? _____

for jewelry? _____

Love

Do you have a mate? _____

Are you single, dating, engaged or married? _____

What is your mate's love map? _____

Is your partner your soulmate? _____

How well do you communicate with your mate? _____

Do you enjoy sex with your spouse? _____

Do you communicate effectively in your relationships? _____

Do you have any children? If so list. _____

How much quantitative and qualitative time do you spend with your
family? _____

Health

How much do you weigh? _____

What size clothing do you wear? _____

What is your cholesterol level? _____

What is your blood pressure? _____

When was the last time you had a physical? _____

What was the result? _____

What are your eating habits? _____

Are you on any medications? _____

Are you taking any natural supplements? _____

Do you have any chronic disease? _____

What is your body fat level or BMI? _____

Do you exercise regularly? _____

Spirituality

What is your relationship with the Divine? _____

Do you meditate? _____

Do you spend time in silence? _____

Do you practice a religion? _____

How often do you congregate with peers? _____

Do you tithe? _____

Are you involved in your community? _____

Do you visualize success? _____

Create an experience in your mind of what it is like to be successful. Include all the details above. What do you see? What do you hear?

Step into the experience and live it as though it is happening right now. What does it feel like?

None of this will matter if you don't put it to use. You have to take right action. Taking the right action constantly and consistently leads to great success. For every action there is a reaction. Reaction suggests an involuntary response such as the knee jerk produced by a doctor tapping on the knee with a medical hammer.

When making decisions, you should never react; stop, think, then act with congruence.

One year goals

Look at your goal list and write down all the goals you want to accomplish in the next year.

Where I am now:

_____

_____

_____

_____

_____

_____

_____

_____

_____

_____

_____

_____

_____

Where I want to be:

_____

_____

_____

_____

_____

_____

_____

_____

_____

_____

_____

_____

_____

Three month goals and action steps

What must happen three months from now to make sure you reach your one year goals?

Three month goals: **One year goals:**

_____   _____

_____   _____

_____   _____

_____   _____

_____   _____

_____   _____

_____   _____

_____   _____

_____   _____

_____   _____

_____   _____

_____   _____

_____   _____

_____   _____

_____   _____

_____   _____

_____   _____

The 30-day outcome

What must happen 30 days from now in order for you to reach your three month goals? This is a key component of your life plan. You must set your 30-day outcome. Once you reach it you must then set another 30-day outcome.

30-day outcome:

_____
_____
_____
_____
_____
_____
_____
_____
_____
_____
_____
_____
_____

Three month goals:

_____
_____
_____
_____
_____
_____
_____
_____
_____
_____
_____
_____

One week goals and action steps

What must happen a week from now to ensure you will reach your 30-day outcome? What steps do you have to take?

Week one goals: **30-day outcome:**

_____   _____

_____   _____

_____   _____

_____   _____

_____   _____

_____   _____

_____   _____

_____   _____

_____   _____

_____   _____

_____   _____

_____   _____

_____   _____

_____   _____

_____   _____

_____   _____

_____   _____

Today

What must I do today in order to meet my one week goals? Where do I start?

Day one goals:

_____

_____

_____

_____

_____

_____

_____

_____

_____

_____

One week goals:

_____

_____

_____

_____

_____

_____

_____

_____

_____

_____

Congratulations! You now hold in your hands a blueprint, a one year plan customized to your needs. You are now better off than more than 80% of the general population. Take the next step and be persistent and consistent in your quest. Make a decision to separate yourself from the crowd. Step up and take responsibility for your own success. You have the tools—now all you have to do is use them.

36

Becoming a Whealth Builder

Creating Infinite Personal Power

+ Think of a situation in your past that caused you pain.

  _____

  _____

  _____

+ Bring up a picture of that situation. Is it a motion picture or a still picture? _____

  If it is a motion picture, make it still.

+ Is the picture in color or black and white? _____

  If it is in color, make it black and white.

+ Is the picture bright, dim or dark? _____

  If it is bright, make it dim or dark.

+ Is the picture close to your face or far away? _____

  If it is close, push it far away.

+ Are there any sounds associated with the picture? Is the sound(s) loud or soft? Near or far? _____

  If there are sounds and they are causing you pain, turn them off.

✦ Are there any feelings associated with the picture? Where in your body are you experiencing those feelings? _____

_____

Turn off any negative physical feelings.

Now, take your black and white, dim or dark picture, which has no sounds or feelings attached to it, and imagine it on the back of a bus traveling very fast on a one way street to infinity.

Do this very fast, in less than two seconds. Watch as the picture gets smaller and smaller and finally disappears with the bus on the one way street never again to come back.

Using Your Personal Power Grid to Forgive and Forget

1. From Self-Power, recall a situation in your past when someone caused you pain and you have been unable to forgive or forget him/her.

2. Bring up a picture of the situation. Step into the picture as though it is happening right now. See, hear and feel what you felt at that moment.

3. Next, shift to Other-Power. Relive the experience from the other person's point of view. See what they saw, hear what they heard. What do you feel?

4. Then, go to Third-Power and become a detached observer watching the situation. What do you see, what do you hear? How does the situation look from this point of view?

5. Move to Integral-Power. Experience the past event as part of the unit. What is the best outcome for the unit?

6. Finally, rise to Infinite-Power. Imagine you are in a rocket leaving the earth. As you get higher and higher in the sky the earth gets smaller and smaller. How does the situation look to you now? How do you feel about it?

7. Now step back to Self-Power. Think of the person you felt caused you pain. How do you now feel about him/her? Can you find it in your heart to forgive that person? Can you forget the pain?

5 Minutes to a Better Day: Enhancing Self-esteem

Write down five great experiences you had today and would like to amplify.

_____

_____

_____

_____

_____

_____

_____

_____

_____

_____

Fully relive the positive experiences. Step into each past experience; see, hear and feel as though you are presently there in the moment. Experience the full emotion of the positive past event.

Non-attachment Through De-layering

Who are you? You might write down your profession, your family, your health, and maybe even your financial standing. But who are you really? Answer this question completely in terms of family, relationships, wealth, health, and spirituality.

Who am I? _____

_____

_____

_____

_____

_____

Imagine you are an onion, a multilayered object. At the center of the onion is the core. Each title listed above represents one of your layers. Now peel the onion layer by layer. As you remove each layer, go inside yourself and determine how you feel about the layer being gone.

Repeat this step until you have removed all the layers and all that is left is the core. How do you feel? Do you like what's there? If yes, enjoy it. If not, find out what it is you need to change.

De-layering is the process used to recognize that you are more than your titles, your possessions, or your behaviors. It is a great tool when used properly. You can use it to remove layers you don't like and replace them with more useful ones. Knowing your "real self" will help you give up unhealthy attachments to people or objects. The brain does not know the difference between real or imagined experiences. It will accept any new programming you give it. You can even de-layer your loved ones or people you do business with. Be safe. Enjoy!

Building Your Daily Mantra

+ Choose the type of day you wish to have.

+ Identify two personal obstacles to your perfect day and state them in positive terms.

+ Identify three resources that you need to make it your desired day.

+ End by accepting responsibility to make today the type of day you want it to be.

Today is a/an _____ day!

I _____

I _____

I _____

I _____

I _____

Because in the end, it is all about me.

Do it now! Go!

The A.U.R.A. of Success

You start by living in the moment, being acutely *aware* of your surroundings, your inner state, and the state of those around you. Then you seek *understanding*, knowing that you delete, distort and generalize outside experiences.

Next you accept *responsibility* knowing it is all about you. None of it is real; it is reality as you experience it. Finally take *action*, the right action. Constantly and consistently pay attention to your intention so you may get your desired result. That, my friends, is the A.U.R.A. of success.

Now go and be successful!

Dream
Believe
Create
Inspire...

APPENDIX

1. _____
2. _____
3. _____
4. _____
5. _____
6. _____
7. _____
8. _____
9. _____
10. _____
11. _____
12. _____
13. _____
14. _____
15. _____
16. _____
17. _____
18. _____
19. _____
20. _____

Notes _____
_____
_____

Use this page to plan your
weekly activities.

Week beginning _____
and ending _____

This week's schedule

Date:

Day 1

_____
_____
_____

Date:

Day 2

_____
_____
_____

Date:

Day 3

_____
_____
_____

Date:

Day 4

_____
_____
_____

Date:

Day 5

_____
_____
_____

Date:

Day 6

_____
_____
_____

Date:

Day 7

_____
_____

My goals for today

1. _____ Intent: _____
2. _____ Intent: _____
3. _____ Intent: _____
4. _____ Intent: _____
5. _____ Intent: _____
6. _____ Intent: _____
7. _____ Intent: _____
8. _____ Intent: _____
9. _____ Intent: _____
10. _____ Intent: _____

Two unwanted outcomes

1. _____
2. _____

Three outstanding outcomes

1. _____ Positive intent: _____
2. _____ Positive intent: _____
3. _____ Positive intent: _____

Daily Notes _____

_____

_____

_____

The A.U.R.A. Practitioner's Diary

Today's date _____

Day _____

Today's weather _____

Temp: HIGH _____ LOW _____

Blood pressure _____

Weight* _____

Heart rate _____

Waist/hip measurements* _____

Blood glucose: A.M. ____ LUNCH ____ P.M. ____

Total hours of sleep _____

Time	Activity	Duration
	Spend time in silence	15 min.
	5 minutes to a better day & daily mantra	5 min.
	Exercise (walking)	30 min.

		Time	Calories
Breakfast			
Snack			
Lunch			
Snack			
Dinner			
		TOTAL CALORIES TODAY	

Time	Activity	Duration
	Plan next day	15 min.
	Spend time in silence	15 min.
	5 minutes to a great weight**	5 min.

* Monitor weekly.   ** Same as 5 minutes to a better day.

*A practical weekend workshop about
getting what you want out of life.*

This 4-step personal development program, AURA,

+ **A**wareness
+ **U**nderstanding
+ **R**esponsibility
+ **A**ction

emphasizes the four pillars of Whealth: Spiritual, Financial, Health and
Love.

Imagine your life just as you want it to be; being at your very best,
standing at the top of your game. Imagine success on your own terms.
What does it look like? What does it sound like? What does it feel like?

Are you living that life now? Are you storming toward your life
dreams? Or are you stuck in a rut, feeling lost and confused?

Maybe you are not even sure what you want out of life.

Imagine that life works the way you want it to be working, having
what you need, getting what you want, being focused, powerful and
ready.

Have you ever wondered why some people seem to do so well in life?
Ever wished you could find out their secret? Well if you did, what would
you do with it? What would you use it for? Where would it take you?

If you are sick and tired of being sick and tired, then I invite you to
come and spend a weekend with me. You are a "can do" person. You are
capable of great things. This workshop will help propel you to the next
level.

You will become skilled at:

+ making more money
+ setting compelling goals

- changing self-limiting beliefs
- moving beyond fears
- generating new behaviors
- losing weight or quitting smoking
- making better sense of your world
- investing in yourself
- curing phobias
- resolving internal conflict
- building deeper and more meaningful relationships
- tapping into your resources
- enhancing self-esteem

Discover new skills, build resources, create new choices and implement them. You will leave feeling energized, invigorated and ready to take action. Most importantly you will leave with a detailed plan ready to put in action.

Whealth Coaching for Peak Performance

So, you have set your goals, identified your obstacles, built resources and now you are ready to leap into action. How do you stay on course? How do you go from tee off to the 18th hole without losing stamina?

A little push or encouragement from a familiar voice at the right time may be just what you need. Coaching provides the perfect means to stay on course, to maintain focus and determination. Your personal peak performance coach will contact you on a weekly basis to ensure continued progress and help as you develop unlimited personal power.

Whealth Builders,™ Inc.
P.O. Box 550548 ■ Jacksonville, FL 32255
800.441.2270 ■ www.willeandre.com

FREE BONUS OFFER

*Help me make history and receive
up to $500 in FREE bonuses*

Thank you sincerely for purchasing a copy of my first book, *Everything is Meaningless*. It is a great compliment and I hope the journey will be worth your time.

I want to give you the opportunity to participate in my Buy-A-Book Save-A-Child Million-in-One World Campaign and earn up to $500 in FREE products and services.

My goal is to become the first self-published, first time author to sell over one million books in one year and help feed 10 million children worldwide.

When you purchase an extra copy of *Everything is Meaningless* for a friend or family member you receive up to $500 in products FREE.

Buy 2+ books, get $100 in bonuses
Buy 5+ books, get $200 in bonuses
Buy 10+ books, get $500 in bonuses

Bonuses include:

+ Free E-books
+ Live Teleseminar
+ One-Day Weekend Event

Plus . . .

I will donate 10% of the purchase price to charity to help fight child hunger around the world. Visit www.buyabooksaveachild.org to learn more.

That's not all . . .

I will match the donation, in effect doubling your gift.

So, order your copies now!
www.buyabooksaveachild.org
www.willeandre.com
or call 800.467.2293

Terms and Conditions

The above described offer is extended to any purchaser of *Everything is Meaningless* (the "Book") who can present an original valid proof of purchase of two or more Books, such as a store receipt, upon registration. Attendance at and participation in the TeleSeminars and the Everything is Meaningless one-day weekend event in Jacksonville, Florida (the "Event") must occur during the twelve (12) months following the date of first publication of the Book. The one-day weekend seminar is limited to the Jacksonville, Florida location. Attendees are responsible for paying for their own travel, lodging and other expenses to attend the Event. Event registration is subject to availability and changes to program schedule. Corporate or organizational purchasers may not use two books to invite more than two people. Participants are encouraged to register promptly @ www.willeandre.com.